Greece & Rome

NEW SURVEYS IN THE CLASSICS No. 35

THE SECOND SOPHISTIC

BY

TIM WHITMARSH

Published for the Classical Association

OXFORD UNIVERSITY PRESS

2005

OXFORD

UNIVERSITY PRESS

Great Clarendon Street, Oxford OX2 6DP

Oxford University Press is a department of the University of Oxford
and furthers the University's aim of excellence in research, scholarship,
and education by publishing worldwide in

Oxford New York

Athens Auckland Bangkok Bogotá Bombay Buenos Aires Calcutta
Cape Town Chennai Dar es Salaam Delhi Florence Hong Kong Istanbul
Karachi Kuala Lumpur Madrid Melbourne Mexico City Mumbai
Nairobi Paris São Paulo Taipei Tokyo Toronto Warsaw
with associated companies in Ibadan

Oxford is a registered trade mark of Oxford University Press
in the UK and in certain other countries

ISSN 0017–3835
ISBN 0–19–856881–9

Typeset by Techset Composition Ltd, Salisbury
Printed in Great Britain
on acid-free paper by
Bell and Bain Ltd, Glasgow

CONTENTS

INTRODUCTION

The Greek literary culture of the first three centuries of our era is no longer viewed as an embarrassing epilogue. It is not just that this is the period of Greek history from which we have the most material (Galen's works alone come close to outweighing the surviving output of classical Athens). Aesthetic values have changed: the Romantic obsession with 'originality' and 'inspiration' has been challenged by newer emphases on 'creative imitation', and indeed (under the influence of postmodernism) the reception, replication, and intertextual refashioning of earlier literary works. Political priorities have also shifted: that Greeks of the period were under Roman occupation is now more likely to inspire sympathetic analyses of colonial politics than dismissive sniffs at a weak and decadent culture. Finally, with all its abundant and frequently exuberant prose literature, the Greek world of the early empire is a wonderful source for those inspired by newer intellectual methodologies, predominantly social and cultural anthropology, gender studies, cultural studies, and the history of sexuality.

The 'Second Sophistic' is a phrase that is used widely, but often in radically divergent senses. This short book begins by exploring what modern scholars mean by the phrase, before turning to address the phenomenon so named by an ancient author, Flavius Philostratus. For Philostratus, the 'Second Sophistic' denoted a constellation of luminous performers who specialized in 'epideictic' oratory. These sophists mixed lurid theatre with intricate scholarship, miming and mimicking figures from the historical past, as well as fictional characters who found themselves in horribly complex moral circumstances. The ambit of Philostratus' 'Second Sophistic' is narrower than that found in many works of modern scholarship. What this book hopes to show, however, is the absolute centrality of display oratory to elite Greek culture of the first centuries of our era. Oratory was not just a gentle pastime of the rich: it was one of the primary means that Greek culture of the period, constrained as it was by Roman rule, had to explore issues of identity, society, family, and power. Although my scope is focused more sharply on oratory, then, I hope that the sweep-shots will be satisfyingly panoramic. Indeed, a concluding chapter (ch. 5) seeks to show how this oratorical culture impacted on the wider literary culture of Roman Greece, concentrating particularly on two features that are central to modern scholarship on the period: the supposed intensification of interest in the self (the inner, private person), and the apparently sudden emergence of prose fiction.

The overall aims of this book are to assess and synthesize the state of various questions in studies of the Second Sophistic (in the narrower sense that I am using), and to open up new interpretations and vistas. I range broadly over a number of issues, from traditional concerns with history, literary analysis, and linguistic and rhetorical theory (ch. 3) to more modern ideas of cultural theory (ch. 2) and the interpretation of texts (ch. 4). I make no apologies for this variety: this is a field that has stimulated some brilliant work across the full spectrum of modern classics. It would be invidious to produce a list of such authors here (they will emerge from footnotes), but it is worth noting that specialist input into studies of the Second Sophistic comes from a huge variety of methodologies (including archaeology, art history, and especially epigraphy) as well as intellectual approaches: perhaps more than any area of ancient literary study, this one really does depend upon a collective (and indeed international) pooling of talent. In a work like this, some parts will inevitably seem derivative to specialists, but I hope there is enough here by way of new material and interpretation to satisfy those exacting judges.

For dates, I use BCE and CE (as equivalents to the Christian BC and AD). Abbreviations are listed in the Bibliography at the end of the book: I highlight here only the two most important, *OSG* for Bernadette Puech's *Orateurs et sophists grecs dans les inscriptions grecs d'époque impériale* (Paris, 2002), and *VS* for Philostratus' *Lives of the Sophists* (*Vitae sophistarum*). For the abundant epigraphic record, I have where possible referred to *OSG*, an indispensable resource, rather listing every scattered edition or re-edition. As is traditional for this series, I have referred the reader to (more or less) accessible works in English in the first instance, but I have also referred to non-anglophone work (particularly in French, German, and Italian) where it is particularly relevant, or where it would be misleading to omit it.

I would like to thank my colleagues at Exeter, generously supported by the Leverhulme Trust, for investing so much energy (and resource) in the study of the post-classical Greek world over the recent past. Stephen Mitchell in particular has helped both directly and indirectly with the content of this book. Many thanks also to Ian McAuslan for his invaluable suggestions and support.

I. THE SECOND SOPHISTIC

This is a book about an extraordinary phenomenon found over all of the Greek-speaking parts of the Roman empire in the first three centuries CE (and some of the Latin-speaking parts, too). In every city worthy of its name, members of the male elite—grown men, and also their younger acolytes—would regularly gather to hear their peers perform oratorical declamations. The aim of these declamations was not to persuade a jury to convict or release a defendant, nor was it to commend a certain course of action to the city. In ancient terms, this was not dikanic (i.e. legal) or symbouleutic (political) oratory, but 'epideictic': the speeches, that is, were delivered for the occasion alone, to solicit the pleasure, admiration, and respect of the audience.[1]

It is hard for moderns to grasp the central cultural importance of this practice without resorting to misleading parallels: pop concerts, sports events, religious gatherings.[2] The audiences at the ancient events were not exercising their consumerist rights over their leisure time or 'witnessing' the power of the divine; they were gathering as members of the educated elite, parading and exercising their status, scrutinizing their peers as their reputations were made and broken, and testing the role of traditional Greek manhood within the demanding environment of imperial aristocratic culture. At once conservative and radical, traditional and innovative, centripetal and centrifugal, the 'Second Sophistic'—I shall argue over the course of this book—offers a new and exciting perspective on ancient literature, one that will be unfamiliar to many readers.

---

[1] The threefold distinction is first aired by Aristotle, *Rhetoric* 1358a–9a. For a general survey of ancient rhetoric, see Kennedy (1994); and more briefly Russell (1981), 114–28. The fullest account of epideictic oratory is Volkmann (1885), 314–61. I do not mean to deny the importance of display oratory in the Hellenistic period: it was certainly practised then (see below, n. 44), but was not apparently socially valued to anything like the same extent (e.g. 'sophist' only appears in this sense as a term of approbation in inscriptions from the time of Trajan (98–117 CE): *OSG*, 6). Later antiquity, again, saw a number of continuities with earlier sophistic culture, with figures such as Libanius, Themistius, and Choricius. Notwithstanding these evident problems, the period between the advent of Augustus and the so-called 'third-century crisis' (much debated, but there does seem to have been a dearth of sophists between the mid-third century and the fourth) is coherent enough a cultural unit to be worthy of exploration.

[2] For these parallels, see e.g. Korenjak (2000), 136.

What is the 'Second Sophistic'?

The 'Second Sophistic' is a widely used phrase: catchy, alliterative, urbane-sounding, and not a little arcane (what exactly is a 'sophistic'?). The question of what it means, though, is more elusive. One of the major works of recent scholarship on imperial Greek literature begins as follows: 'This book is concerned with Greek culture and society between AD 50 and 250, the period known to us from the biographer and sophist Philostratus as the "second sophistic" '.[3] Another is entitled *The Second Sophistic: a Cultural Phenomenon in the Roman Empire*.[4] Still another is subtitled *On the Socio-political Function of the Second Sophistic in the Greek World of the Roman Empire*.[5] What is immediately evident is that all three scholars are using the phrase in different ways: to refer, respectively, to a historical period, to a literary *Zeitgeist* within this period, and to the imperial-Greek habit of oratorical declamation that I identified above.[6]

There is, then, no strong consensus among modern scholars as to what the Second Sophistic is, beyond a vague sense that it is localized in the Greek culture of the first three centuries CE. So where does the term come from? At some point in the late 230s, Flavius Philostratus, a Greek intellectual who will occupy us repeatedly throughout this book, wrote a work called the *Lives of the Sophists*; he dedicated this to a Gordian, perhaps the man who would become the emperor Gordian I (whose regency, shared with Gordian II, did not outlive 238 CE).[7] According to Philostratus, sophists can be divided into two categories, those who practise the 'first sophistic' and those who practise the 'second sophistic' (481; also 507).[8] (We shall return presently to the question of what a 'sophist' is.) The luminaries of the 'first sophistic'—Philostratus cites Gorgias, Critias, and others—treated, we are told, abstract philosophical themes. The second wave, however, involved the delivery of declamations in the guise of other figures.

For the inventor of the phrase, the 'second sophistic' is simply a form of display oratory invented by the fourth-century BCE orator

[3] Swain (1996), 1.

[4] Anderson (1993).

[5] Schmitz (1997), my translation.

[6] For some of the problems of definition, see Anderson (1990).

[7] See Bowersock (1969), 7–8; Nutton (1970); Avotins (1978); Anderson (1986), 297–8; Flinterman (1995), 26–7. Jones (2002) argues, however, for Gordian III. The state of the evidence simply will not permit any certainty.

[8] For fuller discussion of the genesis of the phrase 'Second Sophistic', see Whitmarsh (2001), 41–5.

Aeschines. There is no strict periodization attached to it, as there is in modern uses of the phrase. For sure, the overwhelming weight of numbers implies that this phenomenon reached its peak of popularity in the second and third centuries CE. Philostratus clearly wants us to think of the Second Sophistic as particularly characteristic of imperial Greece. The next practitioner of the 'second sophistic' after the fourth-century Aeschines, chronologically speaking, is Nicetes of Smyrna, who practised at the time of Nero (*Lives of the Sophists* 511–12); Philostratus explicitly passes over the apparently inept figures of the intervening period (named and shamed are Ariobarzanes of Chios, Xenophron of Sicily, and Peithagoras of Cyrene: 510–11). But it clearly matters greatly to Philostratus to root the movement he describes, and indeed names, in the prestigious tradition of classical Athens; to limit the Second Sophistic to the imperial period does a certain amount of violence to his project.

At one level, these are trivial points. It does not matter particularly that modern thought uses a term differently to ancient; indeed, I myself am not claiming any greater authority in my use of the term in this book, which is itself confined to the period of the early Roman empire (poor Aeschines does not feature here). Nor is there any difficulty in the fact that modern scholars themselves differ as to what it means. No one owns language: it is within anyone's gift to redefine terms. Moreover, attempts to come up with absolutist definitions of literary genres, move-ments, and cultures are rarely successful, and almost without exception desperately uninteresting. What *is* problematic, though, is the ascription, explicit or implicit, of the term 'second sophistic' to Philostratus: this gives a misleading impression that we are seeing the world through 'auth-entically' ancient categories, uninflected by the culture-specific demands of the modern academy. If we are going to appropriate and reuse an ancient term, it behoves us to clarify the ways in which our own cultural politics have contributed towards reshaping it.

To understand any feature of the ancient world, we also need to explore the modern history of research into the discipline, and grasp *how* and *why* its contours have been established as they have been. Let us leave Philostratus' definition to one side, and attempt to unpick some of the central issues that have shaped modern conceptions of the Second Sophistic; as we do so, we shall discover a fascinating micro-history of the nineteenth, twentieth, and twenty-first centuries, as well as the intellectual assumptions that still undergird much research into the field today.

Inventing the Second Sophistic

Philostratus' term was first resuscitated in late nineteenth-century Germany. In 1886, Erwin Rohde—a distinguished classicist, and a friend of the young Friedrich Nietzsche—published an article with a title that translates into English as 'Asian rhetoric and the Second Sophistic'.[9] For Rohde (as indeed for Nietzsche), the story of Greek literature was one of steady decline into frigid mannerism. The 'Asian rhetoric' of his title was the sonorous and rhythmical style that we can detect in a range of oratorical works of the period; Rohde called it elsewhere 'the more weakly and effeminate sister' of the traditional, 'Attic' style of oratory.[10] In Rohde's view, *die zweite Sophistik* was a late, and ultimately ineffectual, rearguard counteraction on behalf of Atticism. The Second Sophistic represented Greek culture's futile attempts to reawaken its own dormant virility. The parallels with Nietzsche's (much more optimistic) views on Wagner's reanimation of the German spirit, are striking.[11]

The embattled concepts of 'Atticism' and 'Asianism' will be discussed in more detail in chapter 3. For now, I want to confine myself to sketching (space forbids any more expansive treatment) the relationship between the emergent field of second-sophistic studies and the romantic and nationalist ideologies of late nineteenth-century Europe. In most of Europe, the great period of nation-building took place in the late eighteenth and early nineteenth centuries: government was centralized and in some cases (and to different degrees) democratized, national educational programmes were introduced, a sense of common citizenship was nurtured. Against this backdrop, romanticism in literature and painting encouraged and explored the aesthetics of (supposedly) national qualities: landscape, labour, 'the people' (in German, *das Volk*). The role of classical education in buttressing these new national politics was decisive, particularly in Germany: thanks to theories about a Dorian invasion from the north during the late bronze age, it was widely held that the ancient Greeks were in fact a Teutonic people. Getting back to the real Greeks—the classical Greeks, of course—was, thus, not just an intellectual quest, but the mission of an entire people.[12]

---

[9] Rohde (1886).
[10] Rohde (1914), 310.
[11] Cf. Nietzsche (1993), 94–8; 110–13.
[12] The best accounts in English of the politics of 19th-century classics concentrate on Great Britain: see Jenkyns (1980); Turner (1981); Stray (1998).

For Rohde and his peers, then, the question of the Greeks' cultural vigour carried with it issues of real contemporary urgency. The story of the Greeks' supposed decline from their pinnacle of achievement in the archaic and classical periods, however, was nothing so simple as a national allegory. The reasons why the Second Sophistic was 'good to think with' lay in precisely the thick, complex knot of irresoluble questions that surrounded it. Was Christianity the solution to the problem of general cultural weakness, or simply another manifestation of it? Was the elite's political dominance over the masses during the Roman period cause for cheer or regret? Did the emergence of technical literary scholarship in the Hellenistic period represent the origins of modern scientific scholarship, or was it part of the explanation for the (as it was thought) bloodless, insipid, etiolated prose of later Greece? Scholars have a remarkable capacity to graft their own preoccupations onto the ancient world: these issues mirror exactly the late nineteenth-century world's preoccupation with questions of religious faith versus science, mass, and elite, and the post-industrial 'mechanization' of culture.

Against this backdrop, Rohde's Second Sophistic emerges as a curious hybrid. On the one hand, the reassertion of proper Hellenism, against (what he saw as) the deleterious effects of eastern influence, represented a commendably strong response to cultural infiltration: it was characterized, he claims, by a 'national-Hellenic element'.[13] On the other hand, the Second Sophistic was, in his eyes, too slavish in its imitation of predecessors and pursuit of rules to match the genuine, spontaneous vitality of earlier classical culture. Rohde's Second Sophistic has all the hallmarks, and anxieties, of the late-nineteenth century German classical industry: both sought to revivify a distant past, to reclaim its rightful heritage, but could only do that through the artificial intermediary of technical scholarship.

Rohde's pioneering studies inspired his student Wilhelm Schmid to a massive work, which is still pretty much authoritative today, on linguistic Atticism in the imperial period; like Rohde, Schmid saw Atticism as a reassertion of traditional Greek values against oriental 'Asianism'.[14] For this generation, however, the debate died in 1900, when the great Prussian philologist Ulrich von Wilamowitz-Möllendorff lent his considerable authority to the view that the Second Sophistic was a fiction; as he shrewdly observed, the evidence for

13   Rohde (1914), 319.
14   Schmid (1887–96).

masses of 'Asianist' orators threatening to overrun Greek culture was limited to a few partisan notices in hostile sources.[15]

Scholarship on individual figures, works, and themes (notably questions around the use of the Attic dialect) continued throughout much of the twentieth century,[16] but it was not until the late 1960s that the concept of the Second Sophistic reemerged as an ideological battleground. In 1969, Glen Bowersock published an epoch-making book, *Greek Sophists in the Roman Empire*.[17] Using the latest techniques of prosopography (the study of individual figures from a variety of sources, principally literary texts and inscriptions), Bowersock collected the evidence from and inscriptions for the sophists, and traced their movements against a rich historical background. Bowersock's argument—put briefly—was that the historical role of the sophists was to serve as mediators between the provincial cities and the imperial centre of the empire. We misread their significance if we look to their texts; it is their actions that count.

Within a short space, the battle-lines for the next phase in the life of the Second Sophistic had been clearly drawn. On the one side, Bowersock, followed by Christopher Jones, gauged the significance of the sophists in terms of their relationship to Rome; on the other, scholars concentrated particularly in Oxford (led by Ewen Bowie, and more recently Simon Swain) saw sophistry as an expression of Hellenism, of Greek identity invigorated specifically in response to the phenomenon of Roman occupation: '[t]o reassure themselves that Greece had a claim comparable to Rome, [Greek literary figures] began to dwell more and more, in their principal cultural activities, on the political greatness of the past'.[18] The opposition between these two sets of approaches has been mobilized by a range of issues (including scholarly methodology); but clearly, at one level, the debate is about the degree of cultural independence that a traditional people can maintain when it finds itself within a new 'global' hegemony. It would be too simplistic to reduce this to a debate between scholars working in north-American and old European universities, but one can certainly

---

[15] Wilamowitz (1900); see also ch. 3.
[16] e.g. Boulanger (1923); Sandbach (1936); Keil (1953); Gerth (1956).
[17] Bowersock (1969).
[18] Bowie (1974), 208–9. See also Bowie (1982). The most substantial statement of this position is Swain (1996). Schmitz (1997) takes a related approach, arguing that the Second Sophistic was a means of enshrining elite Greek privilege: his primary area of interest is, however, in the tension between Greek mass and Greek elite, rather than (as with Bowie and Swain) Greek and Roman.

see here late modernity's characteristic concern with the relative ben-
efits of international centralization (industrialization, wealth-creation)
and the maintenance of cultural autonomy at the local level.

In a more recent, parallel development, the Second Sophistic has
been reappraised by critics working in the post-structuralist tradition
as a positive term: 'sophistic' has been aligned with literary sophistication, and 'secondariness' with intertextuality, allusiveness, and literary self-consciousness.[19] For scholars working in this field,
theatricality, performance, playfulness, and elusiveness have become
indicators not of debased values but of a flourishing, energized
culture reflecting actively, if giddily, on its own heritage. Here it is
not modernity so much as postmodernism that is mirrored in accounts
of the Second Sophistic, now the haunt of knowing, arch hyperintel-
lectuals. Scholars, as we have already had cause to note, have a habit
of finding themselves in the Second Sophistic.

Other developments have helped to shape debates over the Second
Sophistic. One is the emergence of gender studies as a recognized
field: not only do we have substantially more evidence for women's
activities, and evidence for greater female mobility in later Greek
culture than in the archaic and classical periods,[20] but also elite
oratory (the 'second sophistic' in the narrower sense in which I am
using it) was dominated by anxieties over manhood.[21] Another is the
removal of some of the hysteria surrounding the historiography of
the early Church, which has meant that Christianity can now be discussed as part of the same cultural and intellectual landscape as the
pagan culture of the Roman east.[22] Still another is the influence of
psychoanalysis, and the desire to probe later Greek philosophy,
dream analysis, and love literature for signs of a new privileging of
the inner self (these topics will be discussed in greater detail in
chapter 5).[23]

This has been no more than the briefest of sketches of the Second
Sophistic's new life in modern academia; it is (necessarily) limited
not only by its broad strokes and omissions, but also by its failure to

---

[19] Cf. Gleason (1995); Connolly (2001); Goldhill ed. (2001); Whitmarsh (2001).

[20] See van Bremen (1996) on the limited evidence. Hallett (1993) argues that the focus
on classical Athens implicitly marginalizes women's history, which is better represented in
later periods.

[21] Gleason (1995). See also ch. 2.

[22] See esp. Brown (1978); Lane Fox (1986); also Perkins (1995) and Cooper (1996) for
discussions of specific topics that range across pagan and Christian.

[23] See ch. 5, 'Writing the self'.

acknowledge the real advances made in our understanding of the period (though this will emerge from my footnotes in the course of our discussion). What it does show, however, is that the Second Sophistic is not simply a phenomenon of the ancient world, lying there like a continent to be mapped out by modern scholarship; it has also been a fertile debating ground for some of the most important issues in the modern West over the last century and more. If we look closely, we have an impressive snapshot of the cultural history of European and north-American intellectual life for a little over a century.

Greece and Rome: a new survey

I want to turn now to explore some of the central issues in modern Second-Sophistic studies, beginning with imperialism and postcolonialism. As we have noted, much twentieth- and twenty-first-century scholarship on the Second Sophistic has been driven by divergent characterizations of the relationship between Rome, the imperial power, and Greece, the colony. As we have also observed, a large factor in this emphasis lies in the modern world's preoccupation with issues such as globalization, imperialism, and postcolonialism. How much did the Second Sophistic owe to the Roman empire?

It is worth recapping briefly how Greece came to be under Roman dominion, though it is a complex story.[24] During what we call the Hellenistic period (c. 330–31 BCE), Roman power expanded across the Mediterranean. Rome was at this time a republic, steered by its patrician senate (who presided primarily over cultural, religious, and internal matters), and particularly by two consuls elected annually from among their number. In the course of the third century, the Romans were preoccupied by war with Carthage.

In the second century, however, they turned their attention eastwards. Alexander the Great's empire, covering Greece, Egypt, and much of the near East, had fragmented into different kingdoms and confederacies. The Macedonian kingdom, centred on northern Greece, was defeated by Rome in the second and third Macedonian wars; the last king, Perseus, was beaten at Pydna in 168 BCE. The 'Achaean league', which dominated southern Greece, was swallowed

---

[24] For more on the historical background of the transition to Roman rule, see Gruen (1984); Alcock (1993), 1–32. For surveys of the literary culture of Roman Greece, see Reardon (1971); Swain (1996); Whitmarsh (2001); (2004a), 139–58.

up by treaty in 146 BCE, an outcome catalysed by the destruction of
Corinth by the general Mummius in the same year. The Seleucid
king Antiochus III, based in Syria, was defeated in Lydia in 190
BCE. King Attalus III of Pergamum (a recently arisen power)
bequeathed his kingdom to the Romans in 133 BCE. This left only
Egypt, which remained independent (although with strong Roman
influence) until 31 BCE, when Octavian defeated Antony and Cleopatra
at the battle of Actium (on the north-western Greek coast). Octavian
agreed to change his name to 'Augustus' and take on the title 'father
of the fatherland', becoming in effect the first emperor.

The Roman annexation of the Greek-speaking world was a protracted
affair. There was no single point of transition from freedom to domina-
tion (though there were of course decisive events). Military force was
certainly employed, and at times pitilessly (Mummius, notably, razed
Corinth to the ground); but much of the process occurred by stealth,
through patronage, treaty, and bequest. Greece, then, became part of
the Roman empire. We need to be careful with our terms, though,
since the word 'empire' contains a fundamental ambiguity. In the
Roman republic, *imperium* referred to the authority invested in an individual in relation to another; the Roman *imperium*, by extension, sig-
nalled Rome's right to govern its subordinate territories. For this
reason, the territories controlled by Rome from the third century BCE
onwards are sometimes referred to as 'the Roman empire'. Yet the
same phrase is also used by anglophone scholars of the chronological
period from the accession of Octavian/Augustus, the first emperor,
until the sack of Rome: in this context, the 'empire' is the polity ruled
by the emperors. The Second Sophistic was 'in' the Roman empire,
in both senses: the sophists patrolled (usually) the eastern cities
subject to Rome, but they also fought for status in the pyramidal
political structure at the apex of which sat the emperor.

The sophists with whom we shall be dealing occupied a complex role
in relation to Roman imperialism. The Romans were masters of the art
of co-opting the goodwill of local elites: the policy of divide and rule
was highly effective. Individual cities, accustomed to a high degree
of self-determination, continued to make political decisions, even if
on a smaller scale. What changed was the superimposition of a layer
of provincial government, overseeing local governance. In this
respect, Greek local and Roman provincial government could almost
be perceived as complementary rather than in tension. From the
Roman point of view, the senator Pliny (CE *c.* 61–112) advises his

friend Maximus, an imperial envoy to Achaea, to allow these sensitive Greeks their pride: 'Never forget that this is the land which gave us law, and not because they conquered us but because we asked for it'.[25] Maximus is to treat the Greeks with respect, sensitivity ... and, of course (this is implicit), authority too.

Roman governance projected itself as a benevolent machine serving the best interests of its subjects (a much-imitated imperialist device), rather than a dominating force. In order to do this effectively, it had to construct a hierarchy of aspirations for the citizens of the East. Peter Brown has described the second and early third centuries CE as an 'age of ambition'—for the aristocrats who dominated the political and cultural landscape of the cities of the Greek east, that is.[26] The gulf between rich and poor, the breadth of which is one of the most obvious characteristics of later antiquity, was already yawning wide by our period. The elite and the would-be elite battled for status, in building monuments, private houses, and public works, in patronizing poets and intellectuals, and (as we shall see) in sophistic performance.[27] This dominant ideal of ambition, of what the Greeks called *philotimia* (and the Romans *ambitio*), provided the vertical framework within which the civic elite competed for the rewards of Roman recognition: citizenship, and thence promotion within the political framework (the number of Greek senators increased swiftly in the second century), and finally imperial acknowledgement, often with posts such as 'Greek secretary' (*ab epistulis Graecis*).[28]

The threat of Roman coercion, however, was dimly perceptible. In his *Political Advice*, Plutarch (CE *c.* 50–118) advises his friend Menemachus (about to enter civic politics) to remember both that he is ruling over free men and that he is subject to Caesar: 'you are subject as well as ruler (*arkhomenos arkheis*) ... you must make your cloak more humble, look out from your office to the proconsul's dais, don't puff yourself up at or trust too much in your crown (you can see the boots over your head)' (813E).[29] The politician should,

---

[25] Pliny, *Letter* 8.24; see Woolf (1994), 118–25 for discussion and further examples.

[26] Brown (1978), 27–53. See also Schmitz (1997), 97–101.

[27] See esp. Hopkins (1965) on the complex and variable criteria for displaying elite credentials.

[28] See in general Bowersock (1969), 30–58; also Lewis (1981); Syme (1982); Schmitz (1997), 50–63; and, on Greek senators, Halfmann (1979). There were also 'chairs' of rhetoric in Athens and Rome: Avotins (1975); Rothe (1989).

[29] On this passage, see Swain (1996), 166, and more generally 161–8; Jones (1971), 110–21; Aalders (1982); Tirelli (1995). For bibliography on Plutarch's political writings, see Whitmarsh (2001), 184–5 n.15.

Plutarch continues, be like actors who 'add their own feelings, character, and reputation to the performance, but listen to the prompter, and do not deviate in their rhythms and metres from the authority granted them by their rulers' (813F).

Education, elitism, and Hellenism

Perhaps the most important of all the arenas for elite ambition was education. Like the English word, the Greek word *paideia* has a double meaning: not just the process of upbringing, but also the property possessed by a select coterie of cultured individuals, the 'educated' (*pepaideumenoi*). Greeks had defined their particular place in the world through claims to superior culture since (at least) the fifth century BCE, the source of the institution of 'general education' (*enkuklios paideia*) comprising literacy, grammar, music, geometry, and (in time) astronomy.[30] The competition for status through learning, moreover, was nothing new: already in the Hellenistic courts we can see clearly visible contests for intellectual dominance, on behalf of both individuals (in e.g., the high-level bickering of the Museum at Alexandria) and states: the Alexandrians, for example, were (according to one commentator, Andron) 'the educators of all the Greeks and barbarians'.[31]

Roman conquest did, however, change the emphasis upon education. According to Roman imperial ideology, culture was the exclusive province of Greece, in a double sense. Firstly, the Greeks were constructed as the sole originators of, and primary experts in, humanist civilization. We have already met Pliny claiming that Greece 'gave us law' (*Letter* 8.24). A better-known example comes in book 6 of Vergil's *Aeneid*, where Anchises advises Aeneas in the underworld that 'others [i.e. the Greeks] may perfect the arts of sculpture, oratory, and astronomy—but you, Roman, remember to rule with empire (*imperium*), these will be *your* arts' (*Aeneid* 6.851–2). This instance directs us towards my second point. Not only was Greece to be conceived of as monopolizing culture, but also its remit was *restricted* to it. Whereas for democratic Athens or Hellenistic Alexandria, for example, culture had been an accessory of power, the Roman imperialist division

---

[30]   See Morgan (1999) for classical Athens, and (1998) for Hellenistic and Roman developments. On the history of *paideia*, see also Marrou (1956); Too ed. (2001); Whitmarsh (2001), 90–130.

[31]   *FGrH* 246 F1 = Athenaeus, *Sophists at Supper* 184b; see further Whitmarsh (2001), 7–8 for the echo of Thucydides 2.41.1.

of labour rigorously apportioned culture to the Greeks and power to the Romans.

Ideological frameworks are there to be manipulated: there are, of course, numerous Roman philosophers and poets (Cicero and Horace being only the most notable examples) who claim to have usurped the primacy in culture traditionally granted to the Greeks. Conversely, and more importantly for our present purposes, it is not hard to find Greeks who excel in both power and *paideia*, by the second century at any rate. The case of Arrian is particularly conspicuous.[32] Flavius Arrianus was at various stages a senator, suffect consul, military commander, and governor of the important frontier province of Cappadocia. He was also the author of (amongst other things) one of our most important sources on the life of Alexander the Great (the *Anabasis*), an updating of (?pseudo-)Xenophon's treatise on hunting with dogs, and a redaction of the diatribes of Epictetus. Lucian refers to him as 'a man among the first rank of the Romans, and a life-long acquaintance of *paideia*' (*Alexander* 2). For this reason, modern scholars sometimes emphasize his junctural cultural status, his position *entre deux mondes*.[33] The weakness of this kind of assessment is that it assumes the inflexibility of the formula associating Greeks with culture and Romans with power. In fact, as a forum for the display of elite ambition, *paideia* could certainly complement the progress of the individual's career; and if the particular individual had chosen a career in Roman politics, displays of *paideia* were only likely to help.[34]

All the same, *paideia* was conceived of as a definitively Greek practice. In Philostratus' *Lives of the Sophists* (*VS*) the followers of the sophists are repeatedly referred to simply as 'the Greeks'. According to Philostratus, one sophist asked another to send 'his Greeks' to visit him, for example; the reply came, 'I shall come myself, along with my Greeks' (*VS* 571). It is not simply in an ethnic sense that these students are Greeks: in studying under great intellectuals, they are learning how to *become* Greeks in the full, cultural meaning of the word.[35] The orator Aelius Aristides, indeed, refers to himself on

---

[32] On Arrian, see esp. Stadter (1980); Vidal-Naquet (1984); Bosworth (1993); Swain (1996), 242–8.

[33] Vidal-Naquet (1984).

[34] It is true, however, that there are relatively few cases in which culture *alone* can be seen to have propelled individuals forward: see Bowie (1982), Lewis (1981), and most recently Schmitz (1997), 50–63.

[35] For 'Greeks' (or similar) meaning students of rhetoric, cf. 531, 564, 567, 571, 574, 588–9, 590–1, 600, 605, 609, 613, 616, 617, 627; also Eunapius, *Lives of the Sophists and*

several occasions as 'the best [or first] of the Greeks'.[36] To practise *paideia* was to strive for a very particular form of identity, a fusion of manliness, elitism, and Greekness.[37] (These ideas will be discussed further in chapter 2.)

In search of the sophist

What kind of *paideia* did the sophists embody? The question is a complex one. Etymologically, the word simply implies a practitioner of *sophia* ('wisdom'), and is found in this sense first in the fifth century BCE. In this context, it is used primarily of a group of travelling intellectuals who taught a range of subjects, from (what we would call) philosophy to rhetoric:[38] men such as Protagoras of Abdera (the originator of the concept of relativism, i.e. that 'man is the measure of all things') and Gorgias of Leontini (known for the ingenuity of his arguments and his sonorous prose). In the late fifth and fourth centuries, however, sophistry became increasingly associated with rhetorical mastery, with the ability to manipulate language for the delectation or persuasion of others.[39] To take just one instance: our earliest extant example of a sophistic text, Gorgias' *Encomium to Helen*, is a dazzling display of persuasive power, arguing (playfully—and, of course, most controversially to the androcentric Athenians) that Helen was not to blame for eloping with Paris. In its crowning argument, the speech self-reflexively suggests that Helen might be exculpated if it was Paris' persuasion that drove her to leave Sparta, since 'language is a mighty potentate' (8).[40] Persuasion is, it goes without saying, the name of Gorgias' game too.

In the eyes of some, however—and this is where the confusion begins—'sophist' became a term of disapprobation. Athenian democracy scorned the technical expertise that could be bought by the rich. In political oratory, 'sophist' quickly became a word with which to besmirch one's opponents with the accusation of self-serving

---

Philosophers 490. The phenomenon is discussed at Rothe (1989), 104; Follet (1991), 206; Anderson (1993), 119; Flinterman (1995), 51.

[36] Aelius Aristides, *Orations* 33.24, 32, 50.87.

[37] See further Whitmarsh (2001), 90–130, with references.

[38] Guthrie (1971); Kerferd (1981).

[39] Cole (1991); Wardy (1996); shorter surveys at Goldhill (2002a), 45–79; Whitmarsh (2004a), 87–105.

[40] Gorgias, frag. 11 DK. For a translation, see Macdowell (1982). According to Philostratus (*VS* 481), Gorgias was the founder of the 'older' sophistic.

disingenuousness: the fourth-century orator Demosthenes, for example, uses it of those who seek to persuade the people through superficial rhetorical trickery rather than the political science he himself claims to have mastered.[41] Aristophanes mocks the 'sophist' Socrates in his play *The Clouds*, where sophistry is presented as a means of evading creditors through persuasion. Conservatives, meanwhile, were no more tolerant, fearing the power of demagoguery. The philosopher Plato, influentially, deploys the term witheringly of those who who seek simply to persuade the mob by any means, rather than seeking the philosophical truth in the rarefied environment of his Academy.[42] For Plato, sophists are untrustworthy not simply because their aim is persuasion rather than reasoned argument, but also because of their association with public performance. The qualitative associations of the term meant that it could never simply *describe* the art and practice of persuasion: sophistry was always bound up with questions of the proper and right way to be an intellectual.

Thanks to its associations with showmanship and smoke-and-mirrors tricksiness, sophistry became increasingly linked with epideictic oratory (we recall that fourth-century theorists introduced the idea of three divisions of oratory: political, legal, and 'epideictic', i.e. occasional, 'showman' performances).[43] When political speech-makers accused their enemies of sophistry, they were charging them with importing the dazzling techniques of epideictic into the more serious arenas of the law-court and the assembly.

This association of sophistry with the public performance of epideictic oratory became canonical; but in the Hellenistic period our narrative breaks off: there are only a few papyrus scraps of Hellenistic rhetoric, not enough to allow for any serious conclusions.[44] When we turn to the first century CE, though, the evidence for vigorous debates over sophistry re-emerges. Scholars debate whether the intel-

---

[41] *On the Crown* 4; 19.246, 250; 29.13, 32; 35.39–40; 59.21; *On Love* 48, 50; fr. 9.1, 13.2. On oratorical uses of the word 'sophist' as abuse, see Hesk (2000), 211–19. Ian McAuslan helpfully notes Disraeli's famous description of Gladstone, in a speech of 1878, as a 'sophistical rhetorician inebriated with the exuberance of his own verbosity'.

[42] Particularly in the *Gorgias* and the *Sophist*.

[43] Above, n. 1.

[44] See esp. Russell (1983), 4; 19–20, citing *P.Hibeh* 15 (= *FGrH* 105A6), *P.Berol.* 9781; also Polybius 12.25a3, 8; 25k8 and Demetrius *On Style* 238 as evidence for the existence of Hellenistic declamation. Brunt (1994), 29–30 notes additionally that Seneca, *Suasoriae* 1–5 cites Greek precedents as well as Roman. As we have already seen, Philostratus (*VS* 510–11) also names the otherwise unknown Ariobarzanes of Cilicia, Xenophron of Sicily and Peithagoras of Cyrene, who practised at some point between Aeschines and Nicetes (who flourished in the mid-first century CE).

lectual and social climate did radically change between the Hellenistic period and the early empire, or whether the apparent shift is simply a function of the evidence available.[45] What concerns me in this book, however, is less the diachronic narrative (i.e. whether things changed between the Hellenistic period and the early empire) than the synchronic context (i.e. the role that sophistry played in imperial Greek society).

The pejorative force found in the word 'sophist' is still very much in evidence in the imperial period, particularly among partisans of philosophy who wish to distance themselves from accusations of flash triviality.[46] The moralist and orator Dio of Prusa (CE *c.* 40–112), for example, uses the term 'sophist' never in a positive, and almost always in a derogatory sense.[47] When he presents himself as the philosophical instructor of the emperor Trajan, to take but one example, he assumes the role of a man who will save the emperor from some 'ignorant and charlatan sophist'.[48] In this instance, though, Dio is doing something more ingenious than simply replicating the Platonic position on sophistry: he is bolstering his own self-presentation as a philosopher specifically by attacking his rivals on the grounds of sophistry (a trick he may well have learned from Demosthenes).[49] This adds a very interesting spin to the question of definition: is Dio a 'real' philosopher in the Platonic mould, the opposite of a sophist? Or is he engaging in performative high jinks, disguising his own sophistic strategies? Ancient commentators were uncertain. Philostratus classifies him among those who 'philosophize in the guise of sophistry' (*VS* 479, 492), men who were not actually sophists, though they seemed to be (*VS* 484).[50] At some point after his death, and presumably before St John, Bishop of Constantinople (*c.* 354–407) received the same title in emulation, his eloquence earned him the sobriquet 'Chrysostom' ('golden mouth'). Basing his view on hints already in Dio's writing, Synesius postulated (rather implausibly) that Dio con-

---

[45] For a sceptical view (unconvincing, to my mind) see Brunt (1994). The limited amount of surviving evidence from the Hellenistic period will confront us repeatedly.

[46] Stanton (1973), 351–8; Brunt (1994), 41–2; 48–50.

[47] *Orations* 12.5, 22.5, 24.3. 34.3, 71.8. See further Stanton (1973), 354.

[48] Dio Chr. 4.33; see more fully Whitmarsh (2001), 192–4. Dio will be discussed in greater detail in ch. 4.

[49] Above, n. 41. According to Philostratus (*VS* 488), Demosthenes' *On the Crown* was one of the texts Dio took with him into exile.

[50] For criticisms of Dio as 'too rhetorical', see also Philostratus, *In Honour of Apollonius of Tyana* 5.40; and *Letters of Apollonius* 9.

verted from sophistry to philosophy during his exile at Domitian's hands.[51] The ninth-century patriarch Photius (*Library* 209/165a) and the eleventh-century lexicon known as the *Suda* (s.v. 'Dio son of Pasicrates, of Prusa') call him a philosopher and a sophist. Though in his writings Dio is at pains to distance himself from the sophists, posterity clearly had more difficulty making the separation. It is likely that contemporaries would have found it equally tough.

When defined against 'philosopher', in the Greek texts of the Roman empire, the term 'sophist' implies fickleness and crowd-pleasing razz-matazz. When defined against 'orator', however, it takes on different inflections. In some circumstances, 'orator' covered the general category of the specialist in rhetoric, while the 'sophist' was a more refined orator, that is to say a famous performer who could command large audiences.[52] On other occasions, however, sophists are distinguished on the basis that they attract students, while orators speak in professional (i.e. legal, political, ambassadorial) contexts.[53] All commentators have recognized the definitional elusiveness of the sophist,[54] but it is worth emphasizing (because the contrary is occasionally maintained) that 'sophist' was certainly not universally regarded as an insult. The very abundance of inscriptional evidence commemorating sophists testifies to this,[55] as does Philostratus' *Lives of the Sophists*.

As an example of the complexity of the term, let us consider briefly the case of Publius Aelius Aristides (CE *c.* 120–81). Aristides is included by Philostratus among his sophists (*VS* 581–5), though he claimed to be an orator not a sophist: not only does he use the term pejoratively on a number of occasions,[56] but also he famously disavows the improvisation that was often thought of as central to sophistic epideixis,[57] and refuses to charge fees to students. In one of his speeches, he distinguishes himself from 'those execrable sophists' (*Oration* 33.29), on the grounds that 'I alone of the Greeks I know have set my hand to speeches not for the sake of wealth, reputation, honour, marriage, or power; I am a pure lover of speeches, and have been fittingly honoured by them' (33.20). Yet even Aristides, who defined

---

[51] Synesius, *Life of Dio*; cf. Moles (1978) for strong suspicion.
[52] Bowersock (1969), 12–15; Bowie (1974), 169 n. 4.
[53] Brunt (1994), 30; Swain (1996), 97–8.
[54] See also Schmitz (1997), 12–13 n.11.
[55] Now conveniently collected in *OSG*.
[56] Stanton (1973), 355.
[57] See below ch. 2, 'The performance'.

himself so powerfully against the sophists (even when delivering declamations that were identifiably sophistic in style), was aware that the
term had multiple meanings. In his speech *Against Plato on the
Four*,[58] he observes the fundamental slipperiness of the term: Isocrates, for example, uses 'sophist' of those engaged in dialectical
debate, and 'philosopher' of public speakers (3.677); while Lysias
calls Aeschines and Plato himself 'sophists' (3.677).

If we are going to get to grips with the ancient conceptualization of
the sophist (to say nothing of hybrids like the 'doctor-sophist'
(*iatrosophistēs*) and the 'dinner-sophist' (*deipnosophistēs*)),[59] then
lexical definitions alone will not suffice. 'Sophistry' was not a fixed
point around which Greek culture organized itself: it was an embattled,
debated term, the meaning and value of which shifted depending upon
the perspective adopted by the speaker in question. It is not worth
trying to erect firm boundaries between the sophistic and the non-
sophistic, in pursuit of some absolute classification. Not for nothing
did Plato compare the sophist to Proteus, the mythical shape-shifting
god:[60] beguiling but endlessly elusive. The crucial issue is the long
history of claim and counterclaim about the core activities of the
sophist, and the evaluation of them; this rich, colourful history is
one of the fundamental reasons why so many intellectuals of the imperial period contributed to the debate.

Sophistry in action

Sophistry, then, was less a single phenomenon than the focus for a
series of debates. If we confine ourselves to the kind of sophistry
described by Philostratus, however, there are some broad contours
that can be traced. Let us begin with the context for sophistic performances. There is some debate as to the size of audiences that sophists
would have played to. For Thomas Schmitz, who considers the

[58] The 'four' are Miltiades, Themistocles, Pericles, and Cimon, the statesmen criticized
in Plato's *Gorgias*.
[59] For *iatrosophistēs*, see *Palatine Anthology* 11.281; *Suda* s.v. 'Gesios'; Bowersock
(1969), 67. For *deipnosophistēs*, see Athenaeus, *Sophists at Supper* (title).
[60] Plato *Euthydemus* 288b; cf. *Euthyphro* 15d, *Ion* 541e; also Philostratus, *In Honour of
Apollonius of Tyana* 1.4, Heliodorus, *Ethiopian Story* 2.24.4. The opportunist philosopher
Peregrinus was also nicknamed 'Proteus': see Lucian's *Peregrinus*, esp. 1; also *Demonax* 21,
Against the Uneducated Book-buyer 14; *VS* 563–4; and *Suda* s.v. 'Philostratus the
Lemnian' (taking Πρωτέα κύνα ἢ σοφιστήν as a single work). See also ch. 5, 'Writing
the self'.

social role of philosophy to have consisted primarily in mediation between mass and elite, the sophists' own frequent claims to have performed before mass audiences are to be believed.[61] Schmitz cites, among other passages, two from Aelius Aristides: 'the council-chamber was so full that it was impossible to see anything but men's heads' (51.32); 'which of us caused more commotion...than I among audiences? Who...affected more of both tribes? I mean both the able and those whom we call the masses?' (34.42). It is unlikely, however, that spaces such as the council-chamber (*bouleuterion*) alluded to by Aristides could physically hold large numbers. Purpose-built sophistic auditoria were also generally small in scale.[62] In response to Schmitz, Hans-Günther Nesselrath observes that the Odeion of Agrippa in Athens, attested as a site of sophistic performance by Philostratus,[63] could only hold 500 people by the mid-second century.[64] It is not impossible that the more stellar figures drew larger audiences (there are stories that some speakers were so brilliant as to attract even those who could not speak the language):[65] theatres and temples are also attested as sites for performance.[66] But the point made by Aristides in the passage is surely that he was exceptional for magnetizing such numbers. Generalization is always rash, but it is on balance more likely that sophistry was usually performed by the elite before an audience consisting primarily of the elite.

Most sophists, as we shall see further in chapter 3, declaimed in Attic, the dialect modelled on that of fifth- and fourth-century Athens.[67] Their speeches were often improvised (see further chapter 2) in response to audience prompts, although they must have been written up afterwards (or beforehand: there is some evidence for cheating, which again we shall consider in chapter 2) to allow for survival. By far the largest group of speeches that survive, or are known of, consists of *meletai* (singular *meletē*). The *meletē* was a speech given in the persona of, or addressed to, a famous figure from myth or ancient history (from the classical period).[68] *Meletai* can be further

[61] Schmitz (1997), esp. 160–8.
[62] Russell (1983), 76.
[63] *VS* 571, 580.
[64] Nesselrath (1998).
[65] *VS* 491 (Favorinus at Rome); cf. 488 (Dio to Trajan).
[66] Russell (1983), 76. For the diversity of spaces for sophistic performance, see Korenjak (2000), 27–33.
[67] For an excellent general account, see Russell (1983).
[68] Reardon (1971), 99–119; Bowie (1974), 168–74; Kennedy (1974); Russell (1983), 1–20; 106–28; Anderson (1993), 55–68; Swain (1996), 90–6; Schmitz (1997), 112–27.

divided into two groups, with the Latin names *suasoriae* (speeches of persuasion or dissuasion, singular *suasoria*) and *controversiae* (fictitious law-court speeches, singular *controversia*). Philostratus' *Lives of the Sophists* contains numerous examples of *meletai*: Marcus of Byzantium, for example, declaimed arguing (in the Doric dialect, suitably) that the Spartans should not take back those who surrendered at the battle of Sphacteria (425 BCE; *VS* 528); Marcus Antonius Polemo of Smyrna delivered speeches with the titles 'Xenophon thinks he should die with Socrates', and 'Solon asks his laws to be rescinded after Pisistratus takes a bodyguard', and three delivered in the person of Demosthenes (*VS* 542). The only surviving rhetorical works of Polemo (a literary heavyweight of the second century) are two *controversiae* in the guise of two Athenian fathers claiming honours for their sons, Cynegirus and Callimachus, after the battle of Marathon (490 BCE).[69] Herodes Atticus—the most famous and richest of second-century sophists, whose benefactions still litter the landscape of modern-day Athens—is even more sparsely represented in the literary record: the one speech that is traditionally attributed to him (though scholars debate the attribution) is a historical *suasoria* set in late fifth-century Larissa.[70] We also have two fragmentary *controversiae* by Hadrian of Tyre and three brief *suasoriae* in the style of Demosthenes by Lesbonax.[71] The best represented producer of sophistic *meletai* is Aelius Aristides, for whom we have 11 extant (*Orations* 5–16).[72]

Other forms of sophistry are represented among the works of Lucian of Samosata (see further chapter 5). His *Encomium of a Fly* is an 'adoxographical' work, praising something that seems at first sight beneath contempt; this genre has its roots in the classical period, with works like Gorgias' *Encomium of Helen* and Isocrates' *Busiris*.[73] The perversity of the situation is exploited with relish: after detailing their enviable martial and sexual exploits, for example, Lucian proceeds to turn the myth that flies are born from the ashes of other flies into a parable for the Platonic view of the immortality of the soul (7; the fly's soul, of course). Assorted introductory speeches (sometimes

[69] Reader (1996). The source text is Herodotus 6.114, but see Reader (1996), 33–40 for other sources and *Nachleben*.
[70] For bibliography on Herodes, see ch. 2, nn. 34–6.
[71] The text of Hadrian's declamations is printed at Hinck (1873), 44–6; Lesbonax is edited by Kiehr (1906).
[72] See Boulanger (1923), 217–93.
[73] Anderson (1994), 171–4; Billerbeck and Zubler (2000), 6–26.

called *prolaliai*) are also found among Lucian's works.[74] His works *Dionysus, Heracles, Amber* or *The Swans, The Dipsads, Herodotus* and *Zeuxis* represent short, chatty narratives that draw comparisons between an anecdotal story and the situation in which the orator currently finds himself.

Notwithstanding the quasi-sophistic moralizing speeches of Plutarch, Dio Chrysostom, Favorinus, and Lucian, this at first sight rather unprepossessing collection represents the aggregate total of sophistic texts transmitted from the second century and its environs. When they are coupled with Philostratus' invaluable *Lives of the Sophists*, and numerous related works (physiognomic, lexicographical, satirical...) in the sophistic orbit, however, we have the foundations of a powerful and compelling case for the proposition that the Second Sophistic was a central medium for second-century Greek culture's self-examination. This is the proposition that we shall probe in the remainder of this book.

---

[74] See Branham (1985); Nesselrath (1990); Anderson (1993), 53–5.

II. SOPHISTIC PERFORMANCE

Performance culture

Imperial Greece was a culture of the written word. Texts were produced and circulated in impressive numbers, in the form of papyrus scrolls and the new technology of the codex book; some were then annotated, illustrated, commented on, or translated. Cities were stuffed with stone inscriptions recording decrees, awards, honours, donations, and commemorations. The imperial bureaucracy was in large part a machinery for the circulation of writing, in the form of edicts, rescripts, and letters.[1] Even the very bodies of slaves were often tattooed. In an increasingly literate world,[2] even those incapable of reading must have sensed the power and burden of the written words that hovered wherever they turned.

The imperial Greek world was, then, a highly textualized culture. And yet it would be highly misleading to suggest that the profusion of writing indicated an erosion of the performance culture of earlier Greece.[3] There is abundant evidence (in the form of inscriptions) for the continuing role of music and song in festivals, for example.[4] Even the emperor Nero, famously, elected to sing at the Olympic and Pythian games (which he rearranged to coincide with his tour of Greece in 67 CE).[5] Hadrian, similarly, played the *cithara* and enjoyed the company of musicians, among them the celebrated Cretan freedman Mesomedes (thirteen poems by whom survive, four with musical notation).[6] Dramatic performances continued, in the form of both truncated classics and new compositions.[7] Smaller-scale dramas could also be found: mimes, for example, or dinner-time shows.[8]

[1] See esp. Millar (1977); and, on literacy and power in the ancient world in general, Bowman and Woolf eds (1994).
[2] See in general Harris (1989).
[3] On classical Athens as a 'performance culture', see Goldhill and Osborne eds (1999).
[4] Bowie (1990), 83–4; Furley and Bremer (2001), 24–5.
[5] Alcock (1994); also Kennell (1988).
[6] *Augustan History, Hadrian* 15.9; see further Whitmarsh (2004b).
[7] See Easterling and Miles (1999), concentrating primarily on later antiquity.
[8] Jones (1991).

Most of all, the performance culture of imperial Greece was dominated by the sophists we encountered in chapter 1: orators who delivered speeches in public before their peers, on a variety of themes. This chapter will explore the idea of sophistry as a specifically performed genre, which differentiates it from the vast majority (if, indeed, not all) of contemporary literature.[9] It is impossible to overestimate the significance of the performance to sophistry: the naked words that we can read today represent only a fragment of the entire communicative package. When fully embodied in performance, the sophist's declamation would have been dynamized by clothing, props, gesture, intonation, vocal texture, complemented by the surroundings, and framed by an ongoing dialogue with the audience.

If we lack any visual evidence, however, we have no shortage of commentary upon their importance. The crucial text here is Philostratus' third-century *Lives of the Sophists*: this collection of minibiographies is crammed with sparkling anecdotes.[10] What we shall see as we explore these issues is that performance is not simply ancillary to the word, but a crucial medium of communicating the identity of the speaker; and, what is more, a forum that allowed the audience to challenge and deflate pretensions. The performance was, in a very real sense, the stuff of the sophistic mission.

The performance

Sophistic performances were tense, nervy affairs. When the superstar Marcus Antonius Polemo saw a gladiator sweating with terror, he commented 'You are in such agony, you must be about to declaim' (*VS* 541). The typical situation that we find in Philostratus is as follows: the sophist appears before the crowd to ask for a theme (*hypothesis*); the crowd selects one (the repertoire being relatively standard), and the orator begins to declaim, perhaps after a moment's reflection.

---

[9] On sophistic performance, see also Anderson (1994), 55–68; Gleason (1995); Gunderson (2000); and esp. Connolly (2001).

[10] On the *Lives of the Sophists*, see Avotins (1978); Anderson (1986), 23–120; Swain (1996), 396–400; Billault (2000), 72–85; Schmitz (forthcoming); Whitmarsh (2004c). On the sources and historical reliability of the text, see Jones (1974), Swain (1991). According to the *Suda* (s.v. 'Philostratus' 1–3) there were three different Philostrati. The question of attribution has raged (see most recently Lannoy (1997)), but it is not in doubt that the author of the *Lives of the Sophists* was Flavius Philostratus, the most important of the Philostrati, and author of *In Honour of Apollonius of Tyana* (see ch. 5): cf. the cross-reference at *VS* 570.

These expectations called for an extraordinary command of both material and language (audiences were most unforgiving towards deviations from classical Attic: see chapter 3), and also a talent for fluent improvisation (*autoskhediazein*).[11] Not all sophists had this skill. One of the greatest, Aelius Aristides, had no talent in improvisation (*VS* 582) and, like his hero Demosthenes, made a virtue of it. Once he even kept Marcus Aurelius waiting while finessing his words. 'Propose the theme today', he said, 'and come to hear me tomorrow. I am a perfecter of speeches, not a vomiter' (*VS* 583).

In general, however, it was indeed in improvisation that the real cachet lay; it was only by extemporizing that these ambassadors of the elite could present themselves as naturally, effortlessly superior.[12] The stakes were high: hesitations, slips, mispronunciations, the accidental or unknowing use of a word that was not *echt*, tedious repetitiousness ... any weakness could expose the sophist to the abuse of his peers in the audience. Philostratus tells a story about Philagrus of Cilicia (whom we shall meet again in this chapter). The acolytes of Herodes Atticus (on whom see further below) heard a rumour that he never improvised on the same theme for a second time, but would declaim (in Philostratus' phrase) 'stale' words. So having invited him to perform on a theme, they mockingly joined in, reading the script along with him; 'uproar and laughter seized the auditorium' (*VS* 579).

The audience, indeed, played a crucial role in the performance. A recent book has argued that ancient sophistry was, fundamentally, a process of two-way communication, a 'dialogue' between speaker and audience.[13] Among other things, audiences cheered, clapped, and even touched and kissed speakers; they also hissed, tutted, and maintained stony silences.[14] Philostratus' story of Philagrus' 'stale' declamations shows us clearly that the significance of sophistry was all about context: the same text could provoke different reactions in different environments. The words of the sophist did not come together into some fixed, eternal monument: more than any other area of ancient literature, sophistic texts gain their meaning from their reception.

The role of the audience, however, was not simply to analyse language and intellectual content, but also to scrutinize the sophist's

---

[11] On improvisation, see Russell (1983), Schmitz (1997), 156–9, Korenjak (2003).
[12] This is the interpretation of Schmitz (1997), 156–9.
[13] Korenjak (2000).
[14] See Korenjak (2000), 68–95.

physical person. The body was the principal site of the issues, and the anxieties, that clustered around sophistic performance. Not for nothing did Polemo cry on his deathbed 'give me a body, and I shall declaim' (*VS* 544).[15] Many ancient authors wrote with half an eye to posterity: 'I have completed a monument more lasting than bronze', writes Horace famously as he concludes his third book of *Odes* (3.30.1). In the sphere of sophistry, though, the disembodied words of the dead count for little: 'all those things you speak of', Herodes is held to have said of his speeches and other achievements, 'are perishable and the prey of time' (*VS* 552). Sophistic declamations gained their meaning, generally, at the time of performance alone.

Sophistic accoutrements

Clothing and physical appearance play crucial roles in sophistic performance. An essay by the satirist Lucian, *The Teacher of Rhetoric*, makes this abundantly clear. This piece is spoken in the voice of a sophistical instructor who advises his students not to bother with difficult material, and to focus instead upon their superficial appearance:

> The most important thing to bring along [to the performance] is ignorance; the next most important thing is recklessness, and then effrontery and lack of shame. Leave at home decency, moderation, and blushing: they are useless, and indeed counterproductive to the matter at hand. But you do also need the ability to shout as loud as possible, a shameless singing voice, and a walk like mine. These are essential; in fact sometimes they are enough on their own. Let your clothes be either colourful or white, the product of Tarentine manufacture, so that they show your body through them. Your sandals should be those of an Attic woman—you know, with lots of sections on them—or else boots from Sicyon, conspicuous with white felt. You should always have lots of attendants and your book to hand. (*Teacher of Rhetoric* 15).

There is a strong current of effeminacy and luxury underlying all this: the lurid clothing, the girly sandals, the felt booties. As so often in Lucian, the emphasis upon the superficial appearance of his targets is counterpointed by the representation (only implicit, in this case) of the satirist as a speaker of unadorned truth.[16] The link between sophistry and superficiality, indeed, is an easy one to make. For Lucian's speaker, the contrived visual appearance is pretty much all that the sophist needs: 'First of all, you must take most care of all

---

[15] An allusion to the saying of Archimedes, 'Give me somewhere to stand and I shall move the world': see Reader (1996), 20.

[16] See e.g. Whitmarsh (2001), 261–3.

over your style and the attractiveness of your dress; then pick fifteen or (at the most) twenty Attic words, and practise them carefully ...' (*Teacher of Rhetoric* 16).

Lucian's satire, of course, depicts sophistry in unforgiving terms: satire is generically predisposed to draw strong lines between good and bad, between effeminate and manly, between integrity and superficiality, between satirist and subject (despite the flagrant hypocrisy: Lucian himself was, after all, a practised sophist).[17] To get a more positive assessment of the role of accoutrement in sophistic performance, we need to look to Philostratus' *Lives of the Sophists*. Alexander 'the Clay Plato', for example, was a native of Seleucia in Cilicia.[18] His mother was extraordinarily beautiful, and looked like a painting of Helen by Eumelus; although he shared his name and talent for oratory with his supposed father, there was a rumour that his real father was the mystical sage (and subject of a different work by Philostratus) Apollonius of Tyana. Alexander certainly had, according to Philostratus, a 'godlike' appearance: a beard with curls like grape-clusters, but moderate of length, large, languid eyes, a well-proportioned nose, the whitest of teeth, and long fingers, appropriate for holding the reins of speech. Not that Alexander's charms were all innate: in a moment of irritation, the emperor Antoninus Pius referred to him as 'the one who is always arranging his hair, brushing his teeth, polishing his nails, and smelling of perfume' (*VS* 571). Alexander—perhaps taking after his unnaturally beautiful mother—was clearly adept at supplementing his natural qualities. And like Lucian, the emperor takes the opportunity to scoff at the sophist's effeminate artifice.[19]

On one occasion, Alexander visited Athens. Alexander asked the famous sophist Herodes Atticus (who was lodged in nearby Marathon) to bring the young Athenians to hear him declaim; Herodes replied that he would, and he would come himself. On the day of the performance, in the Odeion of Agrippa,[20] Alexander waited for Herodes. When the crowd became restless, he decided to speak. Philostratus' description of the performance exemplifies brilliantly the importance

[17] See also Gunderson (2000), 149–83, with 161–2 on this passage.
[18] On this passage, see further Russell (1983), 84–6; Anderson (1994), 57–9.
[19] Comparable is the spat between the hirstute Timocrates and Scopelian, 'who had given himself to pitch [used for depilation] and hair-removers' (*VS* 536).
[20] On which see ch. 1, 'Sophistry in action'. On Herodes' late arrival, see Korenjak (2000), 73.

of timing, deportment, style, dress, and adaptability to the context. Let us take it episode by episode:

His prologue (*dialexis*) consisted in a series of praises of Athens, and a defence speech addressed to the Athenians against the charge of not having previously visited them. It was of appropriate length, and it was like the epitome of a Panathenaic speech.[21] The Athenians thought he was so well turned out that even before he had spoken a murmur went around praising his good style. (*VS* 572)

Alexander begins his performance by 'praising' Athens; the audience reciprocates with 'praise' (Philostratus uses the same root, *epain-*, in both cases). The audience, however, is impressed not so much by his words as his appearance. Philostratus plays upon this paradox: the word that I have translated 'good style' in the passage above, *to euskhēmon*, might refer equally well to literary as to (as in this case) sartorial style. Alexander is clearly highly aware of the importance of visual effect.

Philostratus continues the narrative by explaining how the audience proposed him a theme on which to improvise, and how Alexander delivered the oration:

The theme that won the audience's approval was: 'A man recalling the Scythians to their nomadic existence, since they are falling ill through living in cities'. Alexander paused for a brief moment (*kairos*); then leapt from his seat, his face beaming, as though bringing good news to those listening to what he had to say. While the speech was proceeding, Herodes appeared, his head covered with an Arcadian cap, as was the fashion in Athens in the summer, perhaps also because he wanted to show Alexander that he was fresh from the road. (*VS* 572)

The theme is proposed by the audience:[22] this will be a live-wire sophistic performance, an improvisation on a topic chosen by the audience. Alexander begins with a theatrical pause for a 'moment': the word Philostratus uses is *kairos*, which implies 'the right time'. The idea that the best sophists have perfect judgement is widespread in the literature of the time (as we shall see in the following chapter). And certainly the beginning seems most skilfully controlled: the pause, then the energetic leap, his facial gestures complementing the theme of the words. What Alexander cannot control, however, is Herodes' entrance: an entrance, moreover, which is every bit as calculated and theatrical as Alexander's own exordium. The cap,

[21] There are extant *Panathenaic Orations* by the 4th-century BCE orator Isocrates and Aelius Aristides (see Oliver (1968)).

[22] This is a relatively common theme: see Apsines, *Art of Rhetoric* 1.48, 72; 2.15; 3.8 (=*RG* pp. 1.339, 342, 351, 355).

Philostratus makes a point of telling us, was not just a fashion statement; it was a coded signal to Alexander that he had travelled from
Marathon to Athens (a journey with a famous history, of course)
especially to hear him declaim.

How did Alexander cope with this challenge? Brilliantly, according
to his biographer: he adapted his speech to incorporate Herodes'
entrance. He then asked Herodes if he would like to hear him continue,
or start afresh with a new one. Herodes asked the audience, who
prompted him to hear 'The Scythians' again; Alexander then reper-
formed the whole speech, 'but with such different language and
rhythm that to those who were hearing him for a second time, he did
not seem to be repeating himself' (*VS* 571). Herodes was mightily
impressed.

Philostratus does quote a few words from the speech to illustrate
Alexander's spectacular ability to rephrase it the second time around.
But these anecdotes emphasize not the permanence of the word so
much as the transience of the performance: Alexander's careful
styling and self-presentation, Herodes' deliberately staged inter-
ruption, Alexander's brilliant rescuing of the situation. The drama
of the occasion turns on a potent mix of the pre-planned (clothing,
gesture) and the unforeseen (the theme proposed, Herodes'
intervention).

Not all sophists were such smart dressers. Marcus of Byzantium was
so scruffy in beard, hair, and appearance that Polemo (on whom see the
following section) thought him a rustic—before he began to speak, at
any rate (*VS* 529). But even Marcus' appearance is a communicative
device, a way of marking out this unusual sophist (who also chose,
exceptionally, to declaim in the Doric dialect rather than the Attic).
Dress was a vital facet of sophistic self-presentation; but as we shall
see repeatedly in other contexts, the most successful practitioners
made their own rules, within the received syntax of sophistic
deportment.

Face, body, signs

We have seen so far that sophistry depends upon performance, with all
its stage props, for its dramatic intensity. Yet there was more at stake in
the sophistic arena than simply the reputations of the pampered elite.
As the passages above demonstrated, this was also a forum in which

issues of gender and identity were fought out: too extravagant a bodily display could be counted as a sign of femininity. Maud Gleason's work, in particular, has demonstrated how the sophist's body became a complex tableau of signs.[23] Gleason identifies a variety of parascientific practices that buttressed this interconnection between gender, the body, and sophistic performance. Chief among them is the art of physiognomics, or decoding character from bodily appearance.[24] A number of physiognomical treatises survive from antiquity, beginning with a tract probably of the third century BCE, the pseudo-Aristotelian *Physiognomics*. The most important, however, was written in the second century CE by Marcus Antonius Polemo of Laodicea, a sophist and figure of huge importance on the Greco-Roman cultural landscape.[25] (The text survives only in Arabic translation, although it also provides the base for a fourth-century anonymous Latin version and an epitome by Adamantius.) It is no coincidence that one of the most significant figures in second-century oratory was also a physiognomist: sophistry, as we have seen, demanded hyperattentiveness to the body and its deportment. These flamboyantly dressed limelight-hoggers inevitably posed serious questions about the behaviour proper to real Greek men.

Let us turn again to Philostratus, and consider this time the case of Hippodromus. This man—a highly successful sophist, who held the chair of rhetoric in Athens—was, according to our author, 'rather rustic in his appearance, though he revealed an amazing nobility in his eyes, his glance being bright and beaming' (*VS* 618). The opposition between appearance and being is culturally coded: 'rustic' is a standard way of designating the subelite, while 'nobility' (the Greek word is *eugeneia*, literally 'excellence of birth') clearly has a social as well as an aesthetic connotation.

In order to exemplify Hippodromus' hidden qualities, Philostratus refers to Megistias of Smyrna, 'deemed second to none among the physiognomists' (*VS* 618). The anecdote that follows is apparently drawn from the writings (now lost) of Megistias. When Hippodromus came to Smyrna and to a temple where Megistias was performing a lecture to his students, he sat down to listen. Megistias asked him what he

---

[23]   Gleason (1995).
[24]   Gleason (1990), reworked as Gleason (1995), 55–81; Barton (1994); see also Hesk (2000), 219–27 on the classical Athenian background.
[25]   Greek, Latin, and Arabic texts of the physiognomic writers can be found in Förster (1893), now reprinted by the University of Michigan Press. A translation of Polemo's *Physiognomics* is forthcoming, by a team led by Simon Swain.

wanted. Hippodromus asked him to swap clothes, since (Philostratus tells us) his was a short mantle (*chlamys*), whereas Megistias was wearing a coat suitable for public speaking (*VS* 619). Once again, we meet the sophists' abiding concern with dress and appearance. But in this case, Hippodromus cuts a much less impressive figure: when he tells Megistias that he aims to give a declamation, Megistias takes him for a madman—until he notices his eyes. Like Alexander in the anecdote we have just discussed, Hippodromus pauses theatrically before leaping up and into his speech, although this only makes Megistias revert to the view that he really is a madman. This time, it is not his eyes but his words that convince him otherwise.[26]

Physiognomy raises complex questions about the relationship between the tension between the individual sophist's innate qualities and the artifices with which he clothes himself. The proof that Hippodromus is not mad lies partly in his eyes, always the primary focus of the physiognomist's gaze, the most legible of the signs of the soul inscribed on the body's surface.[27] But even Megistias, the best physiognomist in the world, cannot decide finally whether he is mad or sane on this basis alone: he has to wait to hear him perform in the sophistic environment before deciding. The individual sign—the glance of the eyes—is not enough by itself to clinch the case. In this anecdote, the role of physiognomics in the scrutiny of the sophists is at best ambiguous.

For Gleason, however, the imprecision of physiognomics (for all the rhetoric of confidence and certainty that one finds in the manuals) is precisely the reason why it was so successful. She cites the case of an apparent contradiction in the sources, whereby fixed, unblinking eyes are as negatively coded as those that move: 'Heads I win, tails you lose; benign behaviour may mask malignant inclinations. Physiognomy puts no one above suspicion. To blink or not to blink, the effect is the same'.[28]

According to Gleason's interpretation, the role of physiognomy is not so much to reach firm conclusions about the nature of the individual as to foster a climate of continual and universal scrutiny; a climate

---

[26] Comparable is the case of Marcus of Byzantium (briefly mentioned above), who 'was unkempt in his beard and hair, as a result of which most people thought him too much of a rustic to be intelligent' (*VS* 529); but 'the character of his brow and the intelligence of his face revealed him a sophist' (*VS* 528). Onomarchus of Andros is another scruffy, rustic-seeming sophist (*VS* 599).

[27] Pseudo-Aristotle, *Physiognomics*. 814b.

[28] Gleason (1995), 57.

which, clearly, depends upon there being precisely *no* certainty as to the true nature of individuals. We might go further, and connect this phenomenon with the long tradition in aristocratic Greek culture of concealing careful scrutiny of individuals behind a pretence of entertainment, notably in the symposium. From earliest times the symposium had been constructed as a space for elite relaxation, but also for the testing of civilized behaviour patterns (*in vino veritas* ...).[29]

The art of physiognomics was a game that any sophist could play, but no one could finally control. As we shall see in the case of prescriptions for language use in the next chapter, sophistry frequently invokes the idea of rules of composition, only to deride those sad individuals who are overly bound by them. Physiognomics, comparably, gave sophistic audiences confidence that there was a decodable syntax of the human body, without decoding it to the extent that a guaranteed recipe for successful deportment could be produced.

Identity parade

All this scrutiny of the body and its clothing seeks to ask what *kind of* person the sophist is. This brings us to a cluster of issues that modern scholarship associates with 'identity'. Identity is a complex and variegated concept, and I do not propose to discuss its multiple meanings here.[30] I shall be using it in a circumscribed sense, to refer collectively and severally to the aspects of a sophist's public image. What matters here, then, is not so much what an individual sophist felt himself to be in private as how his performance in the public sphere was coded by his peers: the two may or may not coincide. Because sophistry was so much a public-performative genre, identities became part of the very fabric of the performance, resources to be manipulated in the service of the show.

We can, broadly, identify three spheres of sophistic identity: gender, culture, and class. These interlock, like the circles on a Venn diagram: the normative ideal of the sophist was simultaneously manly, Hellenic, and noble. 'It is by training', writes a fourth-century CE philosopher, 'that humans differ from beasts, Greeks from foreigners, free men from household slaves, and philosophers from ordinary people'

---

[29] See e.g. Whitmarsh (2004a), 52–67.

[30] See Rutherford ed. (1990) for an introduction to these ideas; further bibliography at Whitmarsh (2001), 35 n.147.

(Iamblichus, *Life of Pythagoras* 44). When asked why he was consorting with the philosopher Apollonius, his acolyte Damis replied (according to Philostratus) 'so that I might seem a wise man instead of an ignorant peasant, an educated man rather than a barbarian' (*In Honour of Apollonius of Tyana* 3.43). *Paideia*, education, created identity: it established the difference between the noble and the subelite, the free and the servile, the Greek and the barbarian—and, we might add, the manly and the effeminate.[31] When Herodes Atticus was once praised for his speech, he replied 'Read Polemo's declamation, and then you will know a *man*' (*VS* 539).[32] Elsewhere, Euodianus is praised because his last words had 'nothing female or ignoble about them' (*VS* 596). Conversely, Aelius Aristides compares some of his peers' oratory to that of a hermaphrodite or eunuch (*Oration* 34.48).

When sophists performed, then, they were parading their identity before their peers. They were also, however, subjecting it to scrutiny. Maud Gleason's work, discussed in the previous section, has shown clearly how vulnerable sophists were to the charge of effeminate behaviour.[33] They could equally well be charged with un-Greek, lower-class, or servile behaviour, although in practice this kind of accusation was more likely to be pitched at the level of linguistic usage than that of bodily deportment. This will be discussed further in chapter 3; for now, I want to limit myself to cases of performance.

Let us begin with the example of Philagrus of Cilicia (*VS* 578–80). Philagrus is pronounced 'brilliant' by Philostratus (578): he reached the highest institutional position possible within sophistry, the chair of rhetoric in Rome. Even so, his achievements were mitigated by his inability to control his fearsome temper. This is visible physiognomically in his countenance: he was short, 'his brow was harsh, and his eye was mobile and quick to anger' (*VS* 581). This irascibility is implicitly coded by Philostratus in cultural terms. When faced by

[31] See further Whitmarsh (2001), 90–130. We have already seen that Philostratus simply uses the phrase 'Greeks' (*Hellēnes*) to designate students of rhetoric (*VS* 571, 588, 613, 617; above, ch. 1 n. 35). The existence of lower-class sophists has been asserted, but is unlikely: see Bowie (1982), 54–5.

[32] For 'the man' used of sophists, see also *VS* 537, 564, 586. A solitary female orator, Aufria, is commemorated in a second-century inscription from Delphi: see *OSG*, 156–7 (n. 53). Another female orator, ? Ioannia, is commemorated in a CE fifth-century funerary stele from Egypt (*OSG*, 315–16).

[33] Gleason (1995); see also Gunderson (2000) and esp. Connolly (2003). Athletics were also a crucial site for testing manliness: see van Nijf (1999), (2001), (2003); and König (forthcoming). On the limited opportunities for women in the imperial Greek world, see van Bremen (1996).

some students of Herodes Atticus in Athens whom he took to be mocking him, the red mist descended, and 'an outlandish (*ekphulon*) word escaped him in his anger' (*VS* 578). This slip from canonical usage—shocking in a sophist—was seized upon by the most talented of the students, who asked him, 'In which of the great authors can that word be found?' (*VS* 579) Philagrus' status as an ambassador of elite Greek identity was at risk; fortunately, he was quick-witted enough to deliver the perfect riposte. 'In Philagrus', he said (*VS* 579).

Identity was not an inner being fixed inside the sophist: it was, rather, linked to his public persona, and shifted with his fortunes. The anecdote above exemplifies this point perfectly. Philagrus— whose name means something like 'rustic-lover'—hails from provincial Cilicia (in southern Asia Minor) and is, hence, a less culturally central figure than the Athenian students he faces. This is his point of maximum vulnerability: indeed, the word *ekphulon* (which I have translated as 'outlandish'), denoting his unfortunate choice of expression, could be taken to indicate that he does not belong to one of the *phulai* or 'tribes' of Athens. Philagrus brilliantly counters the challenging by asserting his own canonical status. Even so, however, that is not the end of it: Philagrus writes to Herodes (whose surname 'Atticus' signals *his* credentials as an Attic purist)[34] complaining about the behaviour of his students. Herodes writes back criticizing his own practice and offering advice; Philagrus either fails to understand or refuses to act on this advice, with the result that his performance in Athens bombs (*VS* 579). The friction between the two sophists is more than a minor spat between two mighty egos (though that it surely is): Philostratus is dramatizing the issues of identity raised when a talented but frustrated provincial clashes with one of the richest and most powerful men in the Greco-Roman world, 'the king of words' (*VS* 586, 598), 'the tongue of Greece' (*VS* 598).[35] In Philostratus' account, Herodes is (as usual) the winner.[36]

---

[34] Herodes' full name was Lucius Vibullius Hipparchus Tiberius Claudius Atticus: the last name commemorates his father, Tiberius Claudius Atticus Herodes, usually known simply as 'Atticus'. The name could in fact be viewed as either Roman or Greek: Solin (2001), 197–8. For Herodes' family, see Spawforth (1980); Ameling (1983), 1.3–35; Tobin (1997), 13–22.

[35] Cf. the description of him by Marcellus of Side as 'the tongue of the Athenians' (*EG* 1046.37 = Ameling (1983), 2.153 no. 146.37); also n.b. the honorific 'son of Greece' (*IG* 2² 3604b.3 = Ameling (1983), 2.94 no. 69.3). For this kind of phrase, see Whitmarsh (2001), 105 n.59.

[36] For Philostratus' privileging of Herodes, see esp. Anderson (1986), 82–4; Swain (1991).

Norm and deviance

To be a successful sophist, clearly, it helped to be aligned with the positive poles in the series of identity oppositions: Greek-barbarian, elite-subelite, manly-unmanly. The problem, however, is that it is extremely difficult to determine absolutely what counts as 'Greek', 'elite', or 'manly' behaviour. As we saw above, Herodes Atticus implicitly wins out as a more cultivated figure than the thuggish Philagrus. Another case, however, is more problematic. In a well-known passage in the *Lives of the Sophists*, Philostratus reports Herodes' dealings with a certain Agathion, a linguistic purist who chooses to live in the Attic countryside on the grounds that

The interior of Attica is a good school for a man who wants to discuss. For the Athenians in the city receive for money young men who come in streams from Thrace and Pontus and the other barbarian tribes, and their own speech is destroyed more than they can improve the speech of their students; whereas the interior is untainted by barbarians, and so its speech and dialect is healthy, and rings with the most supreme Attic.
(*VS* 553)[37]

Herodes himself had a villa in 'the interior' of Attica, at Marathon, where Agathion lived: to an extent, then, the anecdote reflects favourably on Herodes. But he was also, of course, an internationalist, with connections across the Mediterranean world—and so was far from the model of isolationist cultural purity represented by Agathion. Which one, then, is the 'true' Greek, the Greco-Roman globe-trotter Herodes, or the pastoralist Agathion? Philostratus does not tell us. Different examples of ideal education coexist within the same text, sometimes in conflict.

What is more, it is not the case that practitioners of traditional elite, manly behaviour are the most successful. Audiences demand innovation as well as familiarity. In the competitive sphere of sophistry, carefully measured doses of exoticism (when fused with a respect for traditional values) could prove highly successful. One of the most celebrated intellectuals of the early second century—a philosopher and a historian as well as a sophist—was Favorinus (*fl.* CE *c.* 120–50).[38] Favorinus was, it seems, born without testicles, which gave him a high-pitched voice and (what ancient writers considered) a feminine

[37] On this passage, see Ameling (1983), 1.155–8; Swain (1996), 80; Schmitz (1997), 190–1; Tobin (1997), 261–3; Whitmarsh (2001), 105–8.
[38] On Favorinus, see Gleason (1995), esp. 3–20; Holford-Strevens (1997); König (2001); Whitmarsh (2001), 118–21, 167–78.

appearance.[39] His rival Polemo wrote in his work on physiognomy that his 'voice was like a woman's, and likewise his extremities and other bodily parts were uniformly soft. Nor did he walk with an upright posture: his joints and limbs were lax'.[40] It is almost certainly Favorinus who is the butt of Lucian's satirical dialogue *The Eunuch*: 'I pray that my own son', runs the punchline, 'has not the intellect or the eloquence but the *balls* for philosophy' (*Eunuch* 13).[41] What is more, he was from Arelate (Arles) in Latin-speaking Gaul, which represented an obstacle for one wishing to make a name in Greek learning. Philostratus famously records the three paradoxes he used to proclaim of himself: 'He was a Gaul, but he Hellenized; he was a eunuch, but had been tried for adultery; he had quarrelled with the emperor, but had survived' (*VS* 489).

And yet Favorinus was an enormously successful and highly regarded figure. He is the hero of Aulus Gellius' second-century *Attic Nights* (a huge repository of learning, in 20 books of Latin): one figure, Caecilius, refers to him as 'the single man in my memory most skilled in both Greek and Roman culture' (20.1.20).[42] (The awe-struck Gellius refers only to his intellect, never to his gender trouble.) In the field of sophistry, he was so successful that, when in Rome, even those who did not understand Greek flocked to hear him (*VS* 491). Herodes Atticus is said to have regarded him as his teacher and father, and to have written to him 'When shall I see you, and when shall I lick around your mouth?' (*VS* 490).[43] His inability to cohere to the expected standards of Greekness and manliness clearly did his sophistic career no harm, and very plausibly enhanced it: after all, it was, according to Philostratus, *he himself* who was flaunting his paradoxical status, not just his detractors.

Favorinus' success, presumably, depended in large part upon precisely his confounding of expectations. Sophistry often privileges

---

[39] Philostratus, *VS* 489.

[40] Polemo, *Physiognomics* in Förster ed. (1893), 1.160–4; this translation from the Arabic is based on Gleason (1995), 7, who also provides the identification of the unnamed subject with Favorinus on the basis of the reference to a eunuch, born without testicles, from the land of the Celts.

[41] Cf. Lucian, *Demonax* 12.

[42] On Aulus Gellius, see Baldwin (1975), and esp. Holford-Strevens (2003); for Favorinus' predominance in Gellius, see Gleason (1995), 148–53; Holford-Strevens (2003), 98–130.

[43] Wright (1921), 25 plausibly identifies this as an allusion to Aristophanes, frag. 598 KA: 'But he [Euripides] in turn licked around the mouth of Sophocles, smeared with honey as it was, as though it were a jar'. That the fragment is preserved by Favorinus' teacher (*VS* 490; Whitmarsh (2001), 137 n.15), Dio Chrysostom (52.17), makes it more likely that the phrase was known to him.

new ideas, as we can see from a quick survey of the texts. Among Lucian's sophistic works, the object or event he describes—and hence the description itself—is often presented as 'innovative': the tyrant's torture-chamber in *Phalaris* is 'innovative' (*kainos*, *Phalaris* 1.11), as are some extravagant baths (*kainos*, *Hippias* 8), the way in which a defendant killed a tyrant (*Tyrannicide* 2, 22), and the madness suffered by a stepmother (*Disowned* 6). In Polemo's first declamation, again, the father of Cynegirus praises his son's hand (the one that clung to a Persian ship even after amputation) with the phrase 'What innovation (*kainon*), a body that can think!' (A.37).

And yet the new is not always embraced so warmly.[44] In Lucian's prologue speech (or *dialexis*)[45] entitled *Zeuxis*, notably, he recounts how he was returning home from a rhetorical display, when a crowd confronted him, praising 'the exotic content and the revolutionary aspect (*neōterismos*)' of his performance (1). 'O the innovation (*kainotēs*),' they proceed. 'Heracles, what paradoxes! He is an inventive man; you couldn't point to anything more novel than his thought!' Lucian pronounces himself disappointed: he would have liked them, he says, also to have praised 'the proper use of language, in conformity with ancient usage, sharp intellect, circumspection, Attic grace, powers of construction, and all-round artfulness' (2).

Like Favorinus, Lucian was an exotic figure, at the levels of both literature and personal identity (he was a native Syrian). What the two share, besides their exoticism, is a concurrently strong sense of the importance of tradition. It is the combination of the two that is crucial. Philostratus comments of Aspasius of Ravenna that 'he praised innovation (*to kainoprepes*), but never fell into bad taste, because he used what he invented with a sense of proportion (*kairos*)' (*VS* 627). Those who innovated needed a strong grasp on this elusive quality, 'proportion'.

Competition

Sophists were not simply vehicles for elite Greek identity: they were also individual agents, struggling against each other to carve out dis-

---

[44] On the constraints imposed by expectations and tradition, see Schmitz (1997), 214–31.

[45] The term *prolaliai* is sometimes used, but it has no ancient authority. On Lucian's prologues in general, see Branham (1985) (also Branham (1989), 38–46); Nesselrath (1990). *Dionysus* and *You are a Prometheus in Words* similarly address audiences who find his work 'innovative' (*Dionysus* 5; *Prometheus* 3–4).

tinctive identities for themselves. It is impossible to reduce the gallery of sophists that we find in the *Lives of the Sophists* to any one single recipe: what Philostratus displays is, rather, a kaleidoscopic array of different attempts to forge distinctive identities within the crowded field of early imperial sophistry.

At the heart of the social role of sophistry lay the concept of competition.[46] Greek culture had always been competitive (or 'agonistic'), presenting numerous opportunities for social aspiration to be satisfied or frustrated through conflict with peers: not only through athletics and warfare (the obvious examples), but also through the lawcourts and state politics, where the winners won, and were seen to win, at the expense of the losers (a phenomenon known as the 'zero-sum game').[47] But the advent of the Roman empire added a new edge to the competitiveness of the Greek aristocracy. The desire for Roman citizenship, and thence for promotion within the hierarchies of government or bureaucracy, while far from universal, certainly represented a powerful motor for personal ambition.

We discussed the context for such ambition, or *philotimia*, in the previous chapter. What were the sophists striving for? The French anthropologist Pierre Bourdieu has written widely on the use of education to mark social 'distinction' in the modern world.[48] For Bourdieu, education is a form of 'symbolic capital', convertible to and from real capital (that is, money), though its roots in economic difference are heavily disguised by an 'institutionally organized and guaranteed misrecognition'.[49] In two recent (independently conceived) discussions, Maud Gleason and Thomas Schmitz have argued powerfully that the sophistic culture of imperial Greece operated according to precisely these principles of distinction.[50] Sophistry, they claim, provided an arena within which aristocrats could compete among themselves for cultural capital: this created the impression of a mobile and meritocratic system of status distribution, while concealing the real social inequities that underlay it.

Philotimia is, in imperial Greek writers, routinely coupled with the word *philonikia*, or 'love of victory'.[51] Contemporary pronunciation, however, made *philonikia* phonologically inseparable from *philoneikia*,

---

[46] Gleason (1995); Schmitz (1997), 97–135.
[47] See esp. Osborne (1985); Winkler (1990), 45–70.
[48] See esp. Bourdieu (1989).
[49] Bourdieu (1977), 171–83, at 171.
[50] Gleason (1995); Schmitz (1997). Philostratus notes the defining importance of *philotimia* to sophistry (*VS* 491).

or 'love of quarrels', and the distinction between the two concepts (as well as the phonemes) is often hard to detect in the texts. It was a very short step indeed from the supposedly noble activity of honour-seeking to disputatious aggression. This disputatious temper is visible everywhere, in the powerful hostilities that flared up between individuals: we have already seen disagreements between Herodes and Philagrus, and between Polemo and Favorinus; there were many more.[52]

These were not, however, simply cases of overinflated egos bouncing against one another. Competition for status was the foundation upon which the entire edifice was built: sophistry was at once a collective celebration of the exclusivity of elite culture, and a forum within which individual members of the elite could vie for personal prominence. The performance itself is frequently imaged as an *agōn*, a 'contest'. This language is pervasive:[53] I shall give just one example. Apollonius of Athens, we are told, 'stripped for the contest (*agōn*)', like a wrestler, against Heraclides (*VS* 601). After hearing Polemo (whose very name means 'warlike') in a lawcourt, Dionysius said 'The athlete has strength, but it does not come from the wrestling-ground' (*VS* 525: presumably implying that the strength came from some less salubrious source).

Sophists even argued with themselves. Already in the fifth century BCE, texts such as the *Dissoi logoi* ('double arguments') taught sophists how to argue the same case from opposite angles. Aelius Aristides has a number of examples of paired *suasoriae* (speeches of persuasion) arguing for opposite courses.[54] In Polemo's two extant speeches, for example, the fathers of Callimachus and Cynegirus (two soldiers who fought at the battle of Marathon in 490 BCE) vie for the honour of speaking the funeral oration, which conventionally went to the father of the soldier who had died fighting most bravely.[55] Militaristic

---

[51] Pollux, e.g., puts them together in his list of words marking aggression (*Onomasticon* 1.178). See also e.g. Xenphon of Ephesus, *Ephesian Story* 1.9.9; Cassius Dio 6.23.4, 28.96.1, 41.53.2 (although the two concepts are explicitly distinguished at 56.40.4); Maximus of Tyre 16.4; Athenaeus, *Sophists at Supper* 17e.

[52] See further Bowersock (1969), 89–100; Anderson (1994), 35–9.

[53] *VS* 526, 580, 601. See further Whitmarsh (2001), 188–90.

[54] Orations 5 and 6 are set in Athens in 413 BCE, and argue for and against the proposition that reinforcements should be sent to Sicily. *Orations* 11–15 deal with the aftermath of the battle of Leuctra (371 BCE): should the Athenians take sides with the Spartans or the Thebans?

[55] For text, translation, and commentary, see Reader (1996), whose referencing system I follow.

language pervades the speech—perhaps unsurprisingly, given the theme, but it is interesting to see how the language is also cross-applied to the contest between the fathers and the virtual contest between their sons. It will be outrageous, comments Callimachus' father, 'if Callimachus is defeated in death' (B2); elsewhere, 'Cynegirus is defeated' by Callimachus (B4). The sons' repeatedly stressed valour, their contributions to the victory over the Persians, become in each case a metaphor for their worthiness to win the sophistical war— even though the real competitor, Polemo, scripts both fathers.

Surviving texts like those of Polemo can show how deeply veined in sophistry was the competitive component. This is why any analysis of the phenomenon must focus on the word in performance. As we have seen throughout this chapter, the sophist's dress, actions, face, and body were crucial elements. They did not simply 'support' the words: they were a fundamental part of the message. It was through performance that sophists battled for status and identity among their peers.

III. THE POLITICS OF LANGUAGE AND STYLE

As we saw in the previous chapter, sophistry was, among other things, a space for competition between individual ambitions within the hierarchy of the Greek aristocracy. When a sophist took to the stage, he sought to impress his audience with the vigour and subtlety of his *paideia* (education, culture); at the same time, though, he exposed himself to real risks: 'face' could be lost much more easily than it could be won.

What forms did this *paideia* take? In this chapter, I want to explore the intellectual apparatus that underlay the speeches themselves. Yet it is not just the theory itself that claims our attention; more decisive than the specific debates over language, style, and presentation themselves (important though these often are) is their larger socio-cultural role. *Why* did the choice between (for example) two near-synonyms matter so greatly? What was at stake in the distinction? What kind of person would you be if you chose one over the other? The hypercritical context of sophistic performance demanded this rigorous attention to *minutiae* precisely because such cultural–political tonnage was attached to them.

There is a further reason for looking beyond technical details into the wider world of cultural practice. The status of technical expertise itself, as we shall see, was liable to be questioned. The authors of technical treatises were not simply transcribing universally accepted cultural norms into written forms, but attempting to prescribe, authoritatively, their own partisan views of what constituted correct practice. Against this backdrop, though, those who really excelled were not those who knew the rule-books by heart: the genuine *virtuosi* were rule-breakers and paradigm-shifters, unwilling to be dictated to by others. Technical knowledge of this kind thus had an ambivalent status, at once prized as the key to success and contemned as the ancillary of the mediocre.

Atticism

Let us begin with language and dialect. The Greek language as spoken by the less educated classes (and presumably by the educated classes too, in certain situations) had changed radically since the classical period: grammar, syntax, and phonology had been simplified to the extent that the 'regular' Greek spoken in the second century CE is considered by some scholars to have been closer to modern than to classical Greek.[1] And yet almost all literature of the period was composed in archaizing language based on the 'Attic' dialect used in Athens of the fifth and fourth centuries BCE.[2] The less extreme version of this archaism is known as the *koinē*, or 'common tongue', a simplified form of Attic popularized by Macedonian dynasts in the Hellenistic period. More exacting, though, were the requirements of 'Atticism', a linguistic trend that took a powerful hold in the second century CE. Atticists brandished with a flourish the classical forms long since discarded by the *koinē*: double tau in the place of double sigma (e.g. *thalatta* for *thalassa*), for example, the optative, the 'deictic' iota (e.g. *tauti* for *tauta*), and characteristically classical-Attic morphologies (e.g. *leōs* for *laos*).[3]

The full picture of dialectal usage under the empire is, as one would expect, more complex than this implies. Some imperial texts (e.g. the Gospels, or Epictetus' philosophy: see below, 'Rejecting Atticism') are composed in a dialect that can be squarely identified as *koinē*; others show all the signs of a coherent and consistent attempt to Atticize (e.g. the works of Lucian and Philostratus); still others, e.g. by Dio Chrysostom, Plutarch, and Galen (to whom we shall return), however, represent something else again, more linguistically ambitious than the regular *koinē* but without the ostentatious archaism of 'full' Atticism. Language use in the second century was a capacious and complex field.

Despite the complexity of actual language use, and the evident difficulty (which we shall see in greater detail below) in deciding absolutely whether a given term is or is not Attic, the distinction between 'high' and 'low' languages was a fundamental organizing polarity in the Greek conceptual universe. (And, indeed, remained so until relatively recently: it was only in the 1980s that the PASOK government decided once and for all to promote 'demotic' Greek at the expense of the classicizing 'pure' form.) The discriminating use of language was the fundamental marker of social identity: it defined whether one belonged

---

[1] For a good general survey of the history of the Greek language, see Horrocks (1997).

[2] Tonnet (1988), 1.313–51; Swain (1996), 43–64; Schmitz (1997), 67–96. This view that Atticism was a *Kunstsprache* (or artfully contrived form of speech) is the modern consensus, against Higgins (1945) who argues that it was an extension of everyday 'standard late Greek'.

[3] Schmid (1887–96) is exhaustive.

to the class of the 'educated' (*pepaideumenoi*), on the one hand, or that of the 'idiots' (*idiōtai*) and 'rustics' (*agroikoi*), on the other. When a Phoenician sailor meets a rural vine-grower in Philostratus' third-century *Heroic Tale*, he is initially bamboozled by his sophisticated Greek: 'How is it that your speech is educated? You do not seem to me to be one of the uneducated' (4.5).[4] The ability to Atticize, however in practice that was defined, was a central and exclusive marker of elite identity.

In other contexts, it was Greekness itself that was thought to be at stake. Verbal slips were routinely castigated as 'barbarisms'; that is, as forms of speech appropriate to a 'barbarian' or non-Greek. Errors at the syntactical level might be styled 'solecisms'—a reference to the uncultured Greek spoken in Soloi, the remote town in Cilicia (that is, the south of modern Turkey).[5]

Sophists, in general, sought to Atticize rigorously. There is hardly a mention of any dialect other than Attic in Philostratus' *Lives of the Sophists*—the case of the Doric-speaking Marcus of Byzantium is a telling exception.[6] Attic is always seen here as the vehicle for cultural purity. In a well-known story, Herodes Atticus' friend Agathion recommends the rural interior of Attica as a better school for the tongue than Athens itself, on the ground that it is 'untainted by barbarians'.[7] The primary threat is seen to lie in mixture, in pollution; hence the best Attic is said to be 'pure'.[8]

Lexicography

What makes a given term 'Attic' or not? Who decides? We have from the period a number of lexica that attempt to define proper usage.[9]

---

[4] On this passage, see further Whitmarsh (2001), 103–6, noting the similar phrase at *Lives of the Sophists* 553.

[5] A number of texts survive *On Barbarism and Solecism*, one by Herodian and others anonymous. See also *RG* 3.9, 11, 44, 59, 85.

[6] For references to the Attic dialect, see *Lives of the Sophists* 490, 503, 509, 553, 568, 592, 594; for Marcus' Doric, see 529.

[7] *Lives of the Sophists* 553; see ch. 2, 'Norm and deviance'. Comparable, too, is the case of Herodes' Indian Autolecythus, who barbarically 'mixes Attic with Indian words' (*Lives of the Sophists* 490).

[8] Cf. Lucian, *How to Write History* 21.

[9] The most notable are those of Harpocration (*Usages of the Ten Orators*), Aelius Dionysius (*Attic Words*), Phrynichus (*Selection of Attic Words and Phrases*; his *Preparation for Sophistry* survives only in fragments), Julius Polydeuces (or 'Pollux': his *Onomasticon* or *Wordbook* survives, although again it is thought to be an abridged version), and Moeris'

Analytical word lists were nothing new in Greek culture: the first was apparently created by Gorgias in the fifth century BCE, and they are common in Hellenistic paraliterature (the most famous example being Philetas' *Unordered Glosses*).[10] What is new with these works is the practical use to which they are put: rather than serving recondite poetics or medicine, for example, most of these works (Pollux' being perhaps an exception) aim to provide a linguistic resource for Atticists, and usually Atticist sophists.

The challenge faced by lexicographers is how to transform the fluidity of language in action into an identifiably regularized system, at both the semantic and the dialectal levels. As regards semantics, let us take an example from Phrynichus' *Preparation for Sophistry*. Phrynichus distinguishes between several words marking the sequential transition from night to day: *orthros* is the end of night, *hē diagelōsē hēmera* ('the smile of day') is first light (and hence the end of *orthros*), *heōs* is the twilight period between *hē diagelōsē hēmera* and the full appearance of the sun (p.93 de Borries). Phrynichus' fine distinctions rest upon the proposition that language is tightly economical, and that lexical divisions exactly mirror those of the world. It is not hard to find exceptions that would seem to counter this proposition, though. Heliodorus' great novel *The Ethiopian Story*, for example, begins with *hē diagelōsē hēmera* (1.1.1), but the following words ('when the sun was beginning to beam down over the peaks') make it transparently clear that he is understanding this as daybreak proper. Is Heliodorus simply using the phrase wrongly, then? Or should we conclude instead that it is the principle of a one-to-one correspondence between words and things that is fallacious?

As for dialect, we might take an example from Moeris. The *Attic Lexicon* consists almost entirely of a list of word-forms that 'the Attics use', followed by those that 'the Greeks use' ('the Greeks', in this context, means 'the other Greeks', i.e. in effect those who employ the *koinē*). Moeris is often right, in broad terms, about Attic morphology; but the problem, again, is that he attempts to impose rigid boundaries on a language system that is highly mobile. Thus he writes of terms for sacrificial victims that 'the Attics use *hiereion*, the Greeks *thuma*' (i 5 = p.199 Hansen); yet *thuma* is in fact used unexotically in the Attic orators,[11] and in the fourth-century Athenian his-

Attic Lexicon. See Swain (1996), 32, n. 35, 51–6; Schmitz (1997), 75–83. Hansen (1998), 36–61 discusses Moeris' precursors in Attic lexicography.
  [10] On Philetas' *Ataktoi glōssai*, see Bing (2003), with further references.
  [11] Aeschines, *Against Ctesiphon* 120; Lycurgus, frags 6.2, 8–9.

torian Philochorus.[12] The attempts of the lexicographers to finalize the rules of Atticism, though often authoritarian, could never be authoritative.

If measured against the standards of modern scientific lexicography, these ancient texts will always fall short in some measure. (Modern lexicography is itself of course driven by cultural imperatives too, though that is a different discussion.)[13] But these are no doubt the wrong standards to set. The emphasis in ancient lexicography is, as we have stressed, not so much on positivist science (the accurate recording of the nature of things) as on practical utility: these fundamentally normative texts are not *describing* language use but *prescribing* it. 'The ignorant', writes Phrynichus of words for 'little pomegranate', 'say *rhoïdion* with the diaeresis; we say *rhoidion*' (*Selection* 223). This example, with its impressive pedantry and brutally parsimonious distinction between 'us' and the ignorant, brilliantly encapsulates what is at stake. The lexicographers write for an audience accustomed to identifying distinctions in social class through differences in the pronunciation of little pomegranates.

The perils of Atticism

Lexica, however, could be the objects of suspicion. In Lucian's satirical portrait, the *Teacher of Rhetoric*, the unscrupulous teacher of the title advises the student to 'pick fifteen, or at least no more than twenty, Attic words from somewhere; practise them hard, have them ready on the end of your tongue—*atta, kaita, mōn, amēgepē, lōste,* and that kind of thing—and drizzle them on every speech, like a sauce' (16). In this context, sophists are being satirized for their calculated, but fundamentally ignorant and pretentious, use of Atticisms: the culinary metaphor associates Atticism with non-essential luxuries rather than wholesome nutrition (a device that is expanded to brilliantly grotesque length in Athenaeus' *Sophists at Supper*).[14] More importantly for our purposes, it testifies to the devastating sarcasm that a sophisticate could conjure in response to an approach to rhetoric weakly founded on the uninspired use of lexicography.

[12] *FGrH* 328 F10.
[13] McArthur (1986).
[14] See Jeanneret (1991); and on Athenaeus, Braund and Wilkins eds (2000).

Lucian's approach to Atticism is as complex as one might expect from this kaleidoscopically varied satirist; his subtle shifts and reorientations represent an excellent guide to the tensions generated in a society that demanded saturation in an archaic dialect.[15] *Lexiphanes* is a dialogue in which the Lexiphanes ('Word-displayer') of the title presents to Lycinus (the other participant in the dialogue, whose name invokes Lucian's own) a rewriting of Plato's *Symposium* compounded of horrendous faux-archaisms. This *Symposium* makes Lucian feel sick—another joke connecting language with comestibles—and a doctor is called to purge Lexiphanes of his bilious language (including the familiar terms *atta, amēgepē,* and *lōste*). At the same time as satirizing others' ugly Atticisms, however, Lucian is displaying his own. Like almost all of the over seventy works securely attributed to him, *Lexiphanes* is composed in elegant Attic. Elsewhere, he represents himself as an expert Atticist: in *The Solecist*, notably, he mocks a self-proclaimed expert for failing to identify some carefully planted solecisms.

The paradox might be provisionally resolved by arguing that what Lucian objects to is not so much Atticism as its excessive use ('hyper-atticism'; cf. *Lexiphanes* 25; *Demonax* 26). Philostratus at one point in the *Lives of the Sophists* praises Critias for Atticizing 'neither immoderately nor exotically, for bad taste in Atticism is barbaric' (503).[16] All well and good, but that simply points us towards a more difficult question: how much is too much? What counts as moderation? The crucial point is that such questions are always up for negotiation. Lucian is an expert player of the game, always ready to redefine the rules to suit his purposes; and, what is more, *he wants us to know that*. That Lucian takes contradictory stances in his satires is not the result of intellectual casualness or lack of moral integrity; rather, it enacts the fundamental principle that the winners in the arena of literary performance are those who refuse to be bound by one set of rules.

Lucian is, of course, aware that he too is vulnerable to attack—not least as a 'barbarian' Syrian by birth, whose Greek was learned relatively late.[17] In one work, *In Defence of a Slip in Greeting*, he responds to the accusation that he accidentally said *hygiaine* ('be healthy') rather

[15] For Lucian on Atticism, see especially Swain (1996), 45–9. For his self-subverting use of personae, see ch. 5, 'Self-description and self-praise'. On the *Lexiphanes*, see Weissenberger (1996).

[16] Philostratus also explicitly criticizes 'hyperatticism': see *Life of Apollonius* 1.17, and his short tract on letter-writing (Kayser (1871), 2.258).

[17] See most conveniently and fully Swain (1996), 298–308.

than *khaire* ('be joyful') when he met a Roman governor in the morning. In another, *The False Critic*, he defends his supposedly 'barbarian' misapplication of the word *apophras*. In both cases, he turns defence into attack, not only by sourcing his own linguistic practice in canonical literature and philosophy, but also by accusing his attackers of pathetic pedantry. The parameters have suddenly shifted: it is now those who follow the rules too mechanically who are stigmatized.

What is particularly interesting about these pieces, finally, is that they are both 'come-backs'. As in several other works (*Defence of 'Portraits', The Fisherman, Apology*), Lucian represents himself responding to others' reactions to his earlier utterances.[18] In the goldfish bowl of contemporary literary society, the evaluation of one's performance does not cease at the moment the words leave one's mouth: status needs to be fought for continually, in dialogue with one's audience. In this respect, Lucian—an accomplished sophist himself, though all we have are of course the written texts—mimics the sophist's ability to respond inventively to his audience's moods (see chapter 2).

Rejecting Atticism

Some, on the other hand, chose to reject Atticism altogether. Epictetus (CE *c.* 55–135), the Stoic philosopher (and freedman), imagines the comments of an interlocutor too struck by the trivialities of dialect: 'Epictetus was a nothing, he committed solecisms and barbarisms' (Arrian, *Dissertations of Epictetus* 3.9.14). Epictetus never uses 'sophist' (or any related word) without the connotation of deception or frivolity;[19] what counts, in his view, is not the linguistic packaging but the conceptual content. At the other end of the century, the prodigious physician Galen (CE *c.* 129–99) is similarly concerned to renounce what he sees as the trivial word-hackery of the Atticists. 'I used the names that people use nowadays', he writes at one point, 'because I consider it better to teach things clearly rather than to Atticize in an old-fashioned way'.[20] And elsewhere: 'I would rather

---

[18] See further ch. 5, 'Autobiographies and apologetics'.
[19] Arrian, *Dissertations of Epictetus* 3.2.11, 3.8.1, 3.21 (title), 3.26.16, 4.5.4. On Epictetus, particularly as a philosopher, see the excellent account of Long (2002), with pp. 12–13 on his relationship to conventional *paideia*; also Schmitz (1997), 87–8.
[20] Galen, *On the Faculties of Food* 3, vol. 6, p. 579 Kühn. Gripes against the Atticists recur in this book: see pp. 580, 584, 641; more generally on Galen's resistance to Atticism, see Swain (1996), 56–62; Schmitz (1997), 80–2.

not find fault with and castigate those who commit solecisms in their speech; for it is better to commit solecisms and barbarisms in one's speech than in one's life . . .'.[21]

In both these cases, an author explicitly rejects Atticism to make a point: the rejection is part of the process of creating an intellectual identity distinct from (what is presented as) the faddish, superficial obsession of contemporary sophistry. And yet neither is quite as simple as it seems. In the case of Galen (who is in fact often rather close to the sophists in his practice),[22] recent writers have observed that he is every bit as preoccupied with correct language and style as the Atticists: he was the author of numerous works on linguistic matters. And, indeed, as Simon Swain notes, 'Galen, who was at all times concerned to advertise his genius, could not . . . simply reject and ignore atticism . . . he himself also had to display his competence in Attic Greek': he himself wrote a lexicon of Attic words, in 48 books.[23]

Epictetus is an equally fascinating example. The words attributed to him are not, in fact, his own; what we have are a series of reconstructions of the master's teaching methods by his pupil, Arrian. Arrian was a rich and powerful man, a future consul and general, and far from the social echelon of Epictetus. He was, in addition, a prodigious writer himself, who composed (amongst other things) one of our most important sources for the life and achievements of Alexander the Great, the *Anabasis of Alexander*.[24] One of the most intriguing aspects of Arrian is his propensity towards literary role-playing. As a writer, politician, and soldier, he assumes the fourth-century BCE writer Xenophon as his model: it is from his literary hero that he takes the title *Anabasis*, as well as that of a different work, *On Hunting with Dogs*. Ancient sources tell us that he liked to be known as 'the new Xenophon';[25] and indeed in one of his own works, he calls himself 'Xenophon' *tout court* (*Arrangement against the Alani* 10, 22).

In the *Dissertations of Epictetus*, Arrian is playing Xenophon again; this time, he is mimicking his classical predecessor's *Memorabilia of Socrates*. So we are left with something of a dilemma: is the rugged prose of the *Dissertations* the authentic language of a freed slave, or

---

[21] Galen, *On the Order of his Own Books*, vol. 19, p. 60 Kühn.
[22] On the sophistical aspects of medicine, see Pearcy (1993); von Staden (1997); also ch. 1, n. 59.
[23] *On the Order of his Own Books*, vol. 19, p. 60 Kühn; Swain (1996), 60; cf. Schmitz (1997), 82.
[24] For Arrian, see ch. 1, n. 32.
[25] Photius, *Library* 58; *Suda* A 3868.

the contrived effect of a master literary impersonator? It is true that the frills-free *koinē* in which Epictetus' thoughts are expressed looks more like the language of a slave than that of a wealthy aristocrat. But Arrian was more than capable of manipulating dialect to literary ends: although most of his work was written in scrupulous Attic, his *Indian Matters* represents an assiduous and largely convincing imitation of Herodotean Ionic.[26] Whether we take this avoidance of Atticism as a natural choice on Epictetus' part or as a contrived stylistic device on Arrian's will depend largely on what we decide we want out of this text (broadly: philosophy or cultural history); but it would certainly be naive to see this as any less informed a stylistic choice than the sophists' deployment of Attic.

As Lucian's example has already taught us, though, one author's criticism of the linguistic practice of others does not necessarily put him in the clear. Rather than seeing dialect as simply the expression of a pre-existing literary identity, we need to see it as a calculated choice in the struggle for intellectual self-definition in this fundamentally competitive world.

Attic style

We have been proceeding so far as though Atticism were simply a matter of dialect, a question of which words and which grammatical forms to choose. In practice, however, matters were more complex. In our earliest (apparent) reference to the phenomenon in the Greek writing of the imperial period,[27] the 'Attic' element in oratory clearly refers to more than narrow grammar and vocabulary. In the preface to a work dating to the period of the emperor Augustus, the rhetorical theorist and historian Dionysius of Halicarnassus (*fl. c.* 30–10 BCE) writes in vigorous terms of the superiority of Attic rhetoric to the new variety:

In the period before us, the philosophical rhetoric was subverted: trampled underfoot, made to suffer terrible insults. Since the death of Alexander of Macedon, it began gradually to waste away and die; in our time, it has all but finally disappeared.

---

[26] For Arrian's informed and self-conscious use of dialect, see Tonnet (1988), 1.313–51, focusing on Atticism; on the Ionic of the *Indian Matters*, see Lightfoot (2003), 93–5.

[27] A pair of titles (*How Attic Emulation Differs from Asian* and *Against the Phrygians*, frags 6, 11 Ofenloch) attributed to Dionysius' contemporary Caecilius, however, indicates that the Attic-Asian contrast was to be found in wider Greek culture too. On the differences between Greek Atticism and Roman (which appears earlier in our sources), see Swain (1996), 21–7.

Another form has usurped its place, unbearable in its theatrical shamelessness, unmanageable, lacking in philosophy or any other freeborn education, secretly manipulating the ignorance of the people . . . It is as though in their houses the one were sitting there, a free, temperate wife, mistress of none of her own property, while the other, a mad prostitute, only there to destroy the household, thought to lord it over all the property, intimidating the other and treating her like shit. Similarly, in every city—and nowhere less than in those that are full of education (that is the worst of all evils)—the ancient, Attic, indigenous Muse has taken on the garb of the dishonoured, exiled from her own property; the other, who arrived yesterday or the day before from one of the pits of Asia (a Mysian, perhaps, or Phrygian, or some Carian horror) has seen fit to set up home in Greek cities, driving the former out from their common property: the ignorant driving out the philosophical, the lunatic driving out the sane. (*On the Ancient Orators* 1)[28]

We shall discuss the metaphor in greater detail presently; for now I wish to focus upon the stylistic opposition between the two kinds of rhetoric: 'the Attic Muse' is defined not in isolation but in opposition to the newcomer from Asia. As so often in Greek culture, the positive term (the self) is constructed as the antithesis of a polar negative. Dionysius is recommending a study of the classical Attic orators (and of his work upon them) as the antidote to the decadent oratory of his day; and it is clear that it is not just the choice of words that irks him about the latter, but a more general (albeit strikingly vague; we shall return to this) concern with meretricious, 'theatrical' style in sophistry. Scholars sometimes posit a historical shift, from this more general, cultural-stylistic Atticism, to the more narrowly lexical Atticism of the second-century lexicographers.[29] There is substance in this proposal (although in fact 'linguistic' Atticism is also extolled already in Dionysius),[30] but the matter bears more discussion.

In the late nineteenth century, Erwin Rohde took Dionysius' assertions literally, as the basis for his theory that the 'Second Sophistic' consisted in a reassertion of Atticism to counter the decadence of widespread Asianism. Rohde's rhetoric, indeed, is remarkably close in tenor, if not in execution, to that of Dionysius: Asianism was the 'more weakly and effeminate daughter of the ancient, glorious, Attic art of oratory'; it was overly concerned with ornamentation and display, and was not 'manly'.[31] Thanks largely to Rohde's interpretation of

---

[28] For an edition of this text with commentary, see Hidber (1996).
[29] See e.g. Swain (1996), 24–7.
[30] See *Lysias* 2, where he commends 'pure' Attic diction as a model for all oratory.
[31] Rohde (1914), 310–12, quoted and discussed at ch. 1, 'Inventing the Second Sophistic'; cf. more fully Rohde (1886). Rohde's position is expanded upon at massive length by Schmid (1887–96).

Dionysius, modern scholars use the term 'Asianism' of the proclivity in imperial Greek texts towards sonorous language and poeticizing rhythms.

As the renowned philologist Ulrich von Wilamowitz-Möllendorff saw, however, the evidence for Asianism as a positive aesthetic creed is very slim.[32] Indeed, in extant Greek literature there is no word *asianizein* or *asianismos* to balance *attikizein* and *attikismos*. Who were the Asianists? Was 'Asianism' simply a convenient slogan (*Schlagwort*, to use Wilamowitz's term) created by the self-appointed guardians of tradition, in the light of Roman anti-orientalist rhetoric in the late republic? We need to be careful when we frame the answer. There certainly are texts that marry musical stylistics to sensuous subject-matter: an excellent example is Longus' *Daphnis and Chloe*, which employs a style identified by ancient theorists as 'sweetness'.[33] In much oratory too, the strategic use of jangling rhythms and melodious assonance plays a crucial role.[34] The phenomenon that we call 'Asianism', then, certainly exists; the problem lies with the term, which both conveys a misleading ring of ancient authority and contains an implicit judgement of linguistic transgression and impropriety.

Dionysius' preface, although probably not intended for oral performance, is a masterfully powerful piece of oratory: in a work designed to teach students how to practise rhetoric, its thundering invective against Asian oratory is a startling example of how to persuade your audience that your position is authoritative. As such, it has proven astonishingly successful: the rhetorical image of a style war between two camps, the Atticists and the Asianists, has not infrequently been taken readily for historical reality. Dionysius' words, however, were not written to guide his readers soberly through the landscape of late-Hellenistic and early imperial Greek oratory (although he was of course an accomplished historian in different environments). As we have seen repeatedly, rhetoric does not simply describe reality, but attempts to control how we perceive it. In the 'zero-sum game' of oratory,[35] status is attained by creating distance between oneself and one's rivals. Dionysius is not simply *reflecting* an established and widely recognized distinction between Attic and Asian oratory, but attempting to *impose* one. After all, Dionysius

[32] Wilamowitz (1900).
[33] Hunter (1983), 84–98.
[34] Norden (1898), 1.367–79.
[35] Ch. 2, 'Competition'.

himself is from Halicarnassus, on the south-western coast of Asia: he of all people needs to work double time to maintain his claim to be the ambassador of Attic values.

What is it that Dionysius is attempting to persuade us of? At one level, clearly, he is attempting to commend his present project to his readership: it is only by following the education template that he sets out that we can save ourselves from the moral and cultural decay of the age. At a deeper level, however, Dionysius is attempting to promote the Augustan revolution as the panacea to Greek decline: the advent of Roman rule, he proceeds to tell us (3), has created the conditions for a renaissance of the old, Attic style. Dionysius is a remarkably pro-Roman author: in his mammoth historical work, the *Roman Antiquities*, he even argues (heterodoxically) that Rome is, intrinsically, a Greek city.[36] We can quickly see, then, the cultural work that is being performed by this contrast between the Attic and the Asian: Augustan Rome, and its oratorical apostle Dionysius, represent the only hope of salvation from the mire of cultural decadence.

Styling the man

What kind of cultural values are at stake in this Attic style? We have already noted that bad Greek is associated with 'barbarism' and the East; but in fact this is only one aspect of a complex set of associations, encompassing social class, political identity, mental state, and (particularly) gender. Let us take a closer look at the metaphorical structure mobilized in the passage cited above. Dionysius opposes the two types of oratory, in fact, according to a highly schematic, conventionalized matrix: eastern versus western; ignorant and theatrical versus philosophical; mad versus sane; anarchic (populist, tyrannical) versus traditional aristocratic; profligate versus thrifty; wanton whore versus chaste wife; arriviste versus indigenous; revolutionary versus established.

This passage tells us a lot about the possibilities of identity-construction through language choice: certain styles of speaking could be marked (provisionally, strategically) as more 'proper', more 'Greek', than others. Examples of this phenomenon abound; I confine myself to two. The first comes from the second-century satirist

---

[36] See esp. Hartog (1991).

Lucian. In his *How to Write History*, he castigates those who mix poetic embellishments into their prose histories: 'it is as though you were to take one of those tough and altogether sturdy athletes and put him in a dyed dress, and a prostitute's make-up, and daub his face with make-up and foundation' (8). Lucian's image appeals to the (supposed) constancy and self-evidence of sexual difference, reinforcing the boundary between proper (manly) and improper (slatternly) prose.

My second example is rather different in form, but similar in implication. In his *Lives of the Sophists*, Philostratus records how the sophist Philiscus of Thessaly bombed when he spoke in a trial before the emperor Caracalla: 'he offended with his walk, he offended with his stance, he seemed unsuitably dressed, his voice was half-female, his language was careless and focused on anything other than the subject-matter' (623). 'Style' is a more catholic quality here, encompassing not just the arrangement of words, but also the deportment and dress of the performer (see chapter 2). Here again, though, we see the same interfusion of aesthetic and a range of cultural markers: Philiscus is bad not only at oratory, but also at manhood and general propriety.

What is particularly interesting, though, is the weight given in both these examples to rather elusive qualities like 'moderation', 'appropriateness', 'suitability'. Philostratus states that Philiscus dresses 'unsuitably'; Lucian immediately proceeds in the following sentences to admit that it is in fact acceptable to introduce some poetic devices, 'on the appropriate occasion ... and moderation should be introduced in the matter' (9). The use of culturally sanctioned polarities (particularly masculine–feminine) suggests a strict and obvious line between proper and improper behaviour; but time and again we find ourselves confronted, in practice, with a much more difficult question of *judgement*. How do we identify the 'moderate' use of poetry in prose? What is 'suitable' dress for a performance before an emperor? In Dionysius' critique of Asianism, too, it is (as we have already observed) very difficult to tell exactly what qualities they are in 'Asianic' oratory that have aggrieved him.

How do we explain this aura of vagueness and non-specificity? Perhaps we can simply ascribe it to the loose thinking and airy moralism that we would expect from unscrupulous and self-serving orators. But there seems to be more to it than that; there is an almost systematic, strategic attempt to avoid disambiguation. The fundamental point may be that, while lexical and stylistic rules are useful for low-level purposes (the education of the young, the stigmatization of the inept), they will not by themselves support the full apparatus of social distinction. Rules can be learned by anyone; what sophistry tests for, however, is not simply rote learning but the kind of under-lying character that can present that material 'appropriately', 'suitably', 'moderately'. Sophistry has the appearance of a system, but depended fundamentally on its ability to disguise the real class warfare going on under the surface.

New styles

In the penumbra of the Second Sophistic, we find a plethora of tech-nical writers theorizing style and the proper organization of rhetorical material. Important names include Hermogenes, Theon, Apsines, Aphthonius, Tryphon, Menander Rhetor; there are also important anonymous texts, principal among them the so-called 'Anonymous Seguerianus', a treatise on political speech-making.[37] The authorial voice in these is usually dogmatic and jussive. The 'Anonymous Seguerianus', for example, is dominated (45 usages) by the gerundive, a grammatical form implying obligation: 'one must know', 'one must say', 'one must divide ...' The author is equally preoccupied with examples from the classical authors. It is easy to conclude, when con-fronted by this kind of prescriptive work, that imperial rhetoric was a conservative and rule-bound discipline. Were there opportunities for innovation within style and language?

The picture is complex. Hermogenes, for example, devotes a con-siderable portion of his work *On Invention* to the question of whether there are hard and fast rules on the matter of innovation.[38] Let us take a passage from the *Art of Rhetoric* preserved among the works of Dionysius of Halicarnassus (but probably a work of the second century CE). The author is discussing occasions when it is per-missible to use linguistic 'innovation' (*kainotēs*) in political oratory:

It is a linguistic inconcinnity when, out of overambitiousness, you use all kinds of words all over the place, with no respect for the proper occasion (*kairos*): I mean, for example, using a word from history, dialectic, or poetry (whether tragedy or

---

[37] For stylistic and rhetorical theory, see especially Russell (1981); Kennedy (1994); Rutherford (1998).

[38] The *Art of Rhetoric* wrongly attributed to Aelius Aristides also frequently commends the use of 'innovation' (1.9.1.2, 1.13.1.7, 1.13.2.1, 2.2.1.17, 2.13.1.24), often linking it with the simple style (*apheleia*: 2.12.1.5, 2.13.1.21, 2.13.1.26).

comedy). This may be a display of education (*paideia*), but it also shows a lack of sophistication in execution ... It is not that a word from dialectic, history, or poetry is impossible in political writing, but one has to understand the proper occasion (*kairos*) for the usage, and also the way to handle it. The proper occasion to use it, as an orator, is in the service of vividness, when the word from poetry, dialectic, or history is more vivid. The way of handling it is to prepare the way for it in advance, and to disguise the innovation (*kainotēs*) of the word by means of familiar words arranged before or after it, and to make the fact that the language is from another genre of oratory relevant; for relevance is enough, and compensates for innovation (*kainotēs*). (*Art of Rhetoric* 10.10 = pp. 366–7 UR)

When a word is imported from a different genre, the resulting 'innovation' raises the stakes. On the one hand, one can achieve an impressive vividness (*enargeia*, 'vividness', is one of the most prized qualities of ancient rhetoric). On the other other hand, the risks are high: it is crucial to have a command of 'the proper occasion' (*kairos*), and of the proper way of handling it.[39] We have seen this phenomenon before: real sophistication in rhetoric consists not just in knowing the rules, but also in understanding how, when, and why to apply them. Even if this author does go some way towards explicating the hidden rules, it is striking how frequently we come across these subtle markers of hidden social distinction.

The dangerous ambiguity attached to innovation can also be seen in two parallel examples from Philostratus' *Lives of the Sophists*. The conclusion on Philiscus of Thessaly (the orator with the effeminate voice, whom we met above) states that he should be admitted, despite his weaknesses, among the front-rank rhetors on the grounds of, among other things, his 'pure use of language and innovative (*kainoprepēs*) sound-effects' (623). It is notable here that praise for innovation is balanced by commendation of his traditional, 'pure' (that is, almost certainly, Attic) language. Aspasius of Ravenna, meanwhile, is said to 'approve of innovation (*to kainoprepes*), but he never fell into bad taste, because he deployed his inventions in due measure' (627). Aspasius manages to get away with introducing new features thanks to those now-familiar servants of the sophist, 'good taste' and 'due measure'.

As we saw in the previous chapter, the sophists' approach to the problem of innovation is largely shaped by the challenges of the particular environment in which they operated: the successful sophist's need to appeal to the audience was moderated by a deeply ingrained distaste for populist measures and the association between Hellenism

---

[39] That sophistry depends upon a command of the *kairos* is a traditional idea: see Russell (1981), 118, on Isocrates 12.33; also Tordesillas (1986).

and traditional conservatism. In the narrower matter of stylistic and rhetorical innovation, the central point is that, as with all such theory, there are no hard and fast rules: it comes down to a matter of judgement. In his discussion of the principles of objection and counter-objection, the theorist Hermogenes (*fl.* late second century CE) introduces the example of someone who says 'one should not innovate'; the counterobjection immediately comes, 'it is appropriate to innovate at suitable times' (*On Invention* 3.16). Each statement has the terse dogmatism of an infrangible rule; as we have seen throughout this chapter, though, rules are often renegotiable in the sphere of sophistry.

Sophistry, as we have stressed throughout, came alive in practice, not theory. The conservatizing tendencies of the handbooks are counterbalanced by the demands for innovation and eccentricity. The handbooks are not firm evidence for a culture congealed in rules and regulations; each was designed to be an active local player in the ongoing struggle for sophistic authority.

IV. READING SOPHISTIC TEXTS

In chapter 2, we saw that performance was an essential component of sophistry: if we consider only the disembodied words of the declamation on the page, we shall not understand the power of sophistry's grip on the Greco-Roman elites of the early empire. In this chapter, I want to turn to the texts that survive, exploring the strategies that we might adopt to unpack the words on the page. It is important, though, not to lose sight of the context, for a highly specific reason. These texts do not envisage themselves as containing some inner core of truth, like a sacred book; they are designed, rather, to have their meanings debated in public space. Sophistry is a profoundly relativizing medium: every assertion is always made in full awareness of the possibility of counterassertion in this competitive forum. As a result, it is impossible to approach the surviving texts simply as documents of their authors' views. What we need instead is a sense of how they would have been received in society, of the rich range of *possibilities* for interpreting them. As we shall discover in the course of this chapter, sophistic texts demand a lively and engaged audience, capable of operating on several levels simultaneously.

Figured speech

For sophists were expert in saying more than one thing at the same time. 'Figured speech' (*logos eskhēmatismenos*), in particular, has preoccupied much modern scholarship.[1] According to ancient rhetorical theory, 'figures' (*skhēmata*) are rhetorical devices (such as puns, irony, rhetorical questions, similes, or periphrases).[2] Rhetorical handbooks concentrate generally upon the use of such figures simply as an adornment of one's work, but it is possible occasionally to glimpse another tradition. In his biography of Polemo, Philostratus chides those who accuse his subject of inability in the field of 'figured themes', pointing to the success of a number of his speeches along

---

[1] Ahl (1984); see also Bartsch (1994); Whitmarsh (1998).

[2] Numerous works on *skhēmata* survive, by among others Alexander Numenius and ps-Herodian: see *RG* 3.9–188, and Hansen (1998), 25; also e.g. ps-Longinus *On the Sublime* 17–29. On concealment in rhetorical theory, see Cronje (1993). The classic discussion of figures is Volkmann (1885), 456–505.

these lines, including *Xenophon Wishes to Die at the Same Time as Socrates* and *Solon Asks for his Laws to be Repealed when Pisistratus Receives a Bodyguard*; also 'three speeches on Demosthenes, in which he denounces himself after Chaeronea, argues that he should be punished with death for the Harpalus business, and recommends that the Athenians should flee to their triremes on Philip's approach' (*VS* 542–3). In these speeches, Philostratus tells us, Polemo's use of figures allowed him to preserve the 'ambiguity' or 'both-sidedness' (*to epamphoteron*) of the theme.[3]

'Figuring', in this case, seems to allow Polemo to say one thing and mean another. Presumably the superficial argument for a given proposal was in fact undermined by an implicit commendation of the exact opposite course. Xenophon does not really want to die with Socrates, Solon does not really want to have his laws repealed, Demosthenes is not really advocating the courses he proposes:[4] in each case, the proposal is indicating the absurdity of the action currently being considered by the people of Athens, and indeed the absurd consequences they will lead to. 'Figuring', in this context, must have involved the use of irony and sarcasm to indicate that the true meaning of the speech is quite the opposite. Scopelian too, Philostratus tells us, 'was excellent at figuring his speech and speaking both-sidedly (*epamphoterōs*)' (*VS* 519).

In what practical contexts would we expect to find such figuring? Let us turn to the treatise *On the Sublime*, sometimes attributed to Longinus:

> It is particularly suspect to play tricks using figures. It encourages the suspicion of a trap, a plot, deviousness. It should be avoided when the speech is addressed to a judge who is authorized to decide a case, and especially to tyrants, kings, rulers, anyone in a position of power; for he will be immediately aggrieved if he is deceived sophistically, like a foolish boy, by the figures of an artful orator ... for that reason the best kind of figure is one that conceals the fact that it is a figure. (17.1)

The author of this tract warns that figures are particularly vexatious to those in power (cf. Demetrius, *On Style* 287–95). For that reason, he argues, one should ... not avoid using figures, but avoid *giving the impression* that one is using them. There is a tacit assumption that addressing the powerful necessarily involves the use of figures; and that, furthermore, figures are closely associated with concealing one's thoughts. This locks into a widespread view of tyrannical power in

---

[3] The phenomenon of figured themes is theorized in detail by ps-Dionysius, *Art of Rhetoric* in his section 'on the use of figures' (*peri eskhēmatismenōn*), pp. 295–358 UR.

[4] The subject of *The Adulterer Revealed* is obscure.

antiquity. The historian Tacitus, for example, praises the emperor Trajan for his age of liberty, in which 'you can think what you like and say what you think' (*Histories* 1.1)—in implicit contrast to life under Domitian, when flattery, subterfuge, and paranoia were widespread.

The link between figured speech and talking to monarchs is borne out in a well-known but still extraordinary passage in Philostratus' *Lives of the Sophists* (560–1).[5] Herodes Atticus was arraigned before Marcus Aurelius on the charge of conspiracy with Lucius Verus against him.[6] Immediately before the trial, however, the daughters of his freedman Alcimedon were killed by a thunderbolt. The grief sent Herodes out of his mind:

When he arrived in court, he launched into slandering the Emperor, and did not even figure his speech, though you would expect one practised in this kind of style to dissemble his own anger. Instead he persisted in speaking, with his tongue unstrangled and naked: 'That is what comes of my hospitality to Lucius, whom you yourself sent! Those are the grounds for judging me, to favour a woman and a three-year-old child!'. (*VS* 561)

'He is sentencing himself to death', comments the praetorian guard in attendance. What is most striking about this passage is its implication that one would *normally* expect an orator to address an emperor with figured speech, with 'strangled tongue'; it is only extreme grief that leads Herodes to this act of romantically[7] suicidal frankness.

What should you say to an emperor?

The kind of speech to be adopted before the most powerful man in the world would clearly have to be of a highly marked kind. The opportunities for sophistic (in the narrow sense) performance before emperors were, however, relatively few: it is telling that the passage above concerns a law-court speech rather than a sophistic declamation.[8] Well-known sophists were, on the other hand, frequently chosen to act as ambassadors

[5] On this passage, see also Millar (1977), 3–12; Papalas (1978); Ahl (1984), 201–2; Anderson (1986), 2–3; Flinterman (1995), 39; Tobin (1997), 1–2.

[6] See Kennell (1997) for the background, and the possible links with an Athenian decree published by Marcus Aurelius.

[7] The episode is indeed a novelistic *topos*: for grieving defendants attempting suicide through self-conviction, see Chariton, *Chaereas and Callirhoe* 1.5.4; Achilles Tatius, *Leucippe and Clitophon* 2.34.6; 7.7. Deliberate 'self-denunciations' (*prosangeliai*) were also a genre of sophistic declamation: see Russell (1983), 35–6.

[8] For the evidence for sophists' interactions with emperors, see Bowersock (1969), 43–58; see also Jones (1971), index s.v. 'embassies' (esp. 43–4, 115).

for their cities: partly for their persuasive eloquence, but partly also because, as members of the elite, they competed for this kind of privilege.[9] Dio of Prusa (one of Philostratus' 'philosophical sophists'), for example, served his city in part through embassies to Rome (*Orations* 40.15, 45.2–3): he had personally interceded with the emperor Trajan, winning from him the right for Prusa to increase its Council by one hundred and to mint its own coins, as well as substantial investment in building work.[10] According to Philostratus, Polemo was greatly honoured by Smyrna for his repeated embassies to emperors: on one occasion, his efforts won the city ten million drachmae from Hadrian (*VS* 531). A Greek's chances of winning over the emperor were substantially improved in the second century, when the successive emperors Hadrian (CE 117–38), Antoninus Pius (138–61) and Marcus Aurelius (161–80) prided themselves upon their receptiveness to Greek intellectual activity.[11] Greek sophists, (as well as other high-status cultural figures such as musicians and athletes), regularly served as intermediaries, shuttling between the local peripheries and the imperial centre.

How should one go about winning the heart of the ruler of the known world? The rhetorical theorist Menander Rhetor, composing in the third century CE, offers some advice: 'a speech to an emperor is an encomium of the emperor. For that reason it will include, by general agreement, an amplification of the emperor's good qualities; but it admits of nothing ambivalent or disputed, because of the extreme splendour of the person in question' (368.1–7).[12] Menander immediately assumes that any speech to an emperor will be a speech of praise; and, consequently, that there will be no room in it for ambiguity. The speech should contain only his 'qualities that are universally acknowledged to be positive' (368.7). Menander is cautioning strongly against the introduction of any 'figuring' into the speech. What is at the root of his fears?

Dio Chrysostom *On Kingship*

Speeches to emperors do survive from antiquity. In the corpus of speeches attributed to Aelius Aristides—the attribution has been

---

[9] See Lewis (1981) for the range of ambassadorial appointments.
[10] Jones (1978), 107–8.
[11] Marcus co-ruled with Lucius Verus (CE 161–9) and Commodus (177–80).
[12] For Menander Rhetor, see Russell and Wilson (1981). Heath (2004) appeared too late to take into account in this book.

doubted, but not universally[13]—we find a speech entitled *To the King*, which praises an unnamed emperor. More interesting for our purposes—because, as we shall see, they have more bite—are four famous speeches (*Orations* 1–4), conventionally named the *Kingship Orations* because supposedly delivered before the emperor Trajan, by Dio of Prusa (CE *c.* 50–120).[14] (This is the Dio whom later ancient critics called Chrysostom, or 'golden mouth'.) In these, particularly in the first and third, many of the conventional features of the imperial encomium (that is, those features that would later be formalized by Menander) can be found.[15] But there is also a good deal of protreptic moralizing about the nature of the good king,[16] some of it surprisingly prickly; and perhaps (as we shall consider) a certain amount of playfulness. These orations are far from colour-by-numbers encomium.

I write that they were 'supposedly' delivered before Trajan because little is certain about their actual delivery. The first and the third speeches are explicitly addressed to emperors (1.5, 1.56; 3.2, 3.3). The second and the fourth represent dramatic scenarios in which a figure (Philip II and Diogenes the Cynic, respectively) advises Alexander the Great on kingship. Because Trajan took Alexander as a model, it is an easy conclusion to reach that these two speeches also represent, allegorically, advice addressed to the emperor, but there are of course risks in that kind of assumption. It is also debatable whether the slippery Dio—elsewhere an expert in theatrical self-presentation[17]—really did perform any or all of his orations before the emperor, or whether this is another of his fictions.[18] In *Oration* 57—apparently a *dialexis* (or prologue) introducing a performance of one of the *Kingship Orations*—Dio claims that he is about to give a repeat performance of 'the words I spoke to the emperor' (57.11). Do we take Dio at face value, and believe that he really did advise emperors? Or do we read

[13] Jones (1972), (1981) (genuine, addressed to Antoninus Pius); Stertz (1979) (rhetorical exercise, 3rd–4th centuries); de Blois (1986) (3rd-century, addressed to Philip the Arab); Librale (1994) (early 2nd-century, addressed to Trajan); Körner (2002) (3rd-century, addressed to Philip the Arab).

[14] On these, see esp. Moles (1990); Swain (1996), 192–7; Whitmarsh (2001), 183–216. The grouping of the four speeches on kingship probably goes back at least to Synesius in the fifth century CE (Whitmarsh (2001), 326).

[15] On the encomiastic aspects, see esp. Jones (1978), 115–23.

[16] There is an abundant ancient tradition on philosophical advice to kings, beginning particularly with Aristotle (see frags 646–7 Rose). For discussion, with further bibliography, see Whitmarsh (2001), 181–3.

[17] See Moles (1978).

[18] Whitmarsh (2001), 325–7 argues for the latter (and see also now Bowie (2002a), 51); Moles (forthcoming) for the former.

this as a fraudulent (perhaps playfully so) boast by a habitual self-publicist?

The implications of this kind of question are far-reaching. For one thing, they relate to our assessment of Dio as an intellectual. Was he a philosopher, giving earnest moral advice to Trajan? Or a sophist, concerned primarily with forging an identity for himself among his fellow Greeks?[19] Does Dio belong at all in a book on the Second Sophistic?[20] These are questions that will, perhaps, never be finally resolved: Dio locates himself uneasily on the cusp between the categories of philosopher and sophist.

Let us consider some examples of the slipperiness of Dio's speeches. The second and fourth orations, as we have mentioned, are not direct addresses to the emperor, but reports of dialogues between Alexander the Great and (respectively) his father, Philip II, and Diogenes the Cynic. Now while it is easy to take Alexander as a front for the prodigious general Trajan, and his interlocutors as fronts for Dio, there is nothing in the speeches themselves that insists on this view.[21] Indeed, it is not clear that any of these figures provide comfortable identifications. The reason for Philip's addressing Alexander is said to be the latter's inability to 'restrain himself' (2.1–2). Philip, for example, is said to 'laugh at' (2.13, 17), 'tease' (2.19), and 'delight in' (2.79) his son; but also to 'marvel' (2.7) and 'come close to anger' (2.16) at him. This paternal mixture of fondness, admiration, and (particularly) vexation at his immature son does not seem quite right for the relationship between a philosopher and the emperor.

The identifications in the fourth oration are even less appropriate. Here, Alexander is presented as 'the most ambitious (*philotimotatos*) and most glory-loving of all men' (4.4), a man dominated by his desire to rule the world. Diogenes' subsequent criticism of Alexander is severe: towards the end, for example, he 'unfurled the sails and began the final part of his speech in a particularly high-minded and fearless way' (4.81). Indeed, so hostile is Diogenes towards Alexander that some critics have thought this oration to be addressed to Domitian (the unpopular emperor who ruled CE 81–96) rather than Trajan.[22]

---

[19] These are broadly the positions of, respectively, Moles ((1990), (forthcoming)) and Whitmarsh (2001), 183–216.

[20] In Bowersock (1969), for example, Dio and Plutarch are said to have 'flourished just on the eve of the Second Sophistic; and although they were not part of it, their lives adumbrated many of its most pronounced characteristics' (112).

[21] Whitmarsh (2001), 204–5.

[22] Höistad (1948), 313–20; Desideri (1978), 283, 287–97.

Even if this speech was delivered directly before Trajan, though, what would he have made of it? Would he have thought that Dio was criticizing him? Or that he was criticizing other rulers, like Domitian? Or even that he was criticizing those pesky philosophers who dare to question their rulers?

This figuring of speech recurs in the orations that are (or claim to be) explicitly addressed to the emperor. It is particularly notable how, although he is greatly occupied with praising, Dio always seems to avoid addressing the emperor directly. In the first oration, he produces a list of qualities characteristic of the 'best king' (1.11–35, at 11). The list is capped with a rather elusive conditional clause: 'If any of these qualities seems to apply to you, then blessed are you in your wise and good nature, and blessed are we who enjoy a share in it' (1.36).[23] How close does the addressee come to the ideal? It is left up to him to decide. In the third oration, analogously: 'So that I may not be charged with flattery by those who would slander me, nor you with wanting to be praised to your face, I shall give my speech on the subject of the best king' (3.25).[24] Again, Dio—with the emperor's best interests at heart, *of course*—avoids explicit evaluation of his addressee's behaviour, preferring instead to leave it up to him to decide how well he matches up.

We shall probably never know whether Dio of Prusa really did deliver the *Kingship Orations* before the emperor, and we shall certainly never know what the emperor himself thought. What these orations do show us, however, is just how slippery speeches (purportedly) addressed to an emperor could be: contrary to the theoretical precepts of Menander Rhetor, 'figured' speech was widely associated with addresses even to emperors who were broadly friendly. It is hard to take these speeches as straightforward praise in the Menandrian mould: as soon as insinuations of 'golden-mouthed' sophistry are in the air, the suspicions creep in, and it becomes extremely difficult to read the philosopher-sophist's intentions. Dio was playing a dangerous game; but it won him undying fame.

Parable and allegory

Dio's speeches present a sharp reminder of just how difficult it is to decode the personae adopted in speeches. Even the first and third

---

[23] Moles (1990), 313; Whitmarsh (2001), 211.
[24] Whitmarsh (2001), 196–7.

Kingship Orations, notionally addressed directly to the emperor, begin with short (but actually rather elusive) allegorical stories, about Timotheus playing the pipes before Alexander the Great (1.1–3) and Socrates commenting on the Persian king's happiness (3.1). Dio is extremely fond of such parables, which usually underscore his moralizing programme.[25] There always remains, however, a degree of uncertainty as to how the exemplum matches up.[26] Indeed, Dio himself is teasingly aware of the problems of parables. One of his dialogues, a reported conversation between Dio and an unnamed interlocutor on the subject of the myth of Deianeira's rape by the centaur Nessus, closes with an objection on the interlocutor's part to the practice:

And somehow or other I have the feeling that the method of some philosophers in dealing with their arguments resembles in a way that of the makers of figurines. For these craftsmen produce a mould, and whatever clay they put into this they form into the shape of the mould; and some of the philosophers before now have proved like that, with the result that whatever myth or story they take in hand, by tearing it to pieces and moulding it to suit their fancy they render it beneficial and suited to philosophy. (60.9)

Dio does not allow himself any comeback: the dialogue simply closes soon after, with this playful commentary on philosophers' manipulation of narratives to their own ends still ringing in the ears.

The inclusion of allegorical narratives is relatively common in sophistic speeches.[27] It is a device that seems to have particularly captivated Lucian. In his 'non-sophistic' (in the narrow sense) works, Lucian is well known for his narrative ability: not only in the exotic pastiche the *True Histories*, but also in the story-trading dialogues *Toxaris* and *The Lover of Lies*.[28] Among his more 'sophistic' works, however, narratives figure equally prominently. In particular, in the prologue speeches (*dialexeis* or *prolaliai*)[29] allegorical stories are recounted that bear on the situation in which the sophist finds

---

[25]   It might be said that the *Kingship Orations* 2 and 4 are entirely parabolic (along with *Oration* 5, the supposed alternative ending of 4). See also *Orations* 7.1–80; 16.10; 17.13–18; 20.19–23; 21.4, 6; 43.4–6; 57; 58; 60.9–10; 62; 66.6; and Saïd (2000), 171–4; Whitmarsh (2004d).

[26]   For the general point, see Goldhill (1994).

[27]   Anderson (1994), 156–70; (2000).

[28]   On the *True Histories*, see esp. Fusillo (1988); Rütten (1997); Georgiadou and Larmour (1998); Möllendorff (2000). On Lucian's narratives generally, see Whitmarsh (2004e).

[29]   The prologue speeches are *Dionysus, Heracles, Electrum, Dipsades, Zeuxis, Herodotus, Harmonides, Scythian*: for bibliography, see ch. 2, n. 45. Parabolic narratives are also found in *On the Hall* 1, *You are a Prometheus in Words* 5, and *The Dream*.

himself. In *Dionysus*, for example, Lucian begins with a story about the Indians underestimating the god Dionysus and his comical-seeming band of followers when they attacked. He then decodes the parable: 'most people undergo a similar experience to those Indians when they confront innovative speeches, like mine' (5). So far so good, although as ever with parables there are questions remaining over the extent of the 'fit' (is Lucian aggressively attacking his audience, as Dionysus did the Indians?).

But Lucian proceeds to tell another story, which is altogether more complex. Near the banks of the Indus river is a grove containing three springs. At an annual festival, the Indians visit it to drink: the boys drink from the spring of the Satyrs, the men from the spring of Pan, and 'those of my age' (the elderly) from that of Silenus (6). It is on the latter group that Lucian focuses. These, we are told, remain silent for a while, before speaking with extraordinary eloquence, until the effects wear off. The most amazing thing is that if they are overtaken by sunset, they leave the story; but they pick it up in the same place when they return the following year (7). What is this all about? 'I refuse to draw the moral,' says Lucian, 'for you can already see how I resemble the story' (8). In broad terms, of course, this is true: like the old men in the story, the elderly Lucian will speak with persuasive suavity. But what of the part about the effects wearing off, and about the ability to pick up the same theme the following year? It is possible that the relevance would be clearer if we knew more about the performance context (e.g. which speech this intro-duced)—but unlikely, I think.[30] The point remains that by ostenta-tiously withholding the key, Lucian is teasing us with the possibility of multiple interpretations of his allegory.[31]

Once we admit that the meanings of such stories can shift around, we shift the responsibility for meaning-making away from the speaker and onto the audience. Of all ancient genres, sophistry most embodies the principle, dear to modern reception theory, that literary significance is activated at the point at which it is received, not the point at which it is transmitted.[32] The importance of this principle will become clearer in the following sections.

---

[30] The speculation that this is a prologue to book II of the *True Stories* is based around this allegorical reference to picking up where one left off. But the *True Stories* was com-posed for reading, not performance (as the prologue makes clear: see 1.1, 1.4). See further Anderson (1976), 262–4.

[31] Nesselrath (1990), 139.

[32] See esp. Martindale (1993).

Reinventing history

The question of how a story about a festival practised by an otherwise unattested Indian tribe relates to Lucian is intriguing, but not perhaps of central cultural importance. Stories about the Greek past, however, were potentially highly combustible. Sophistic declamations in persona (*meletai*), as we saw in chapter 1, are usually split into two categories, using the Latin words *suasoriae* (protreptic speeches) and *controversiae* (quasi-legal speeches). Both types of declamation could be based around either historical or fictitious figures; fictitious scenarios are sometimes referred to with the Greek word *plasmata*. In public performance, however, the historical variety predominates (as opposed to learning and practising exercises, where fictitious characters were more likely to be used).[33] Most of these speeches are now lost, but it is interesting to note the extraordinary prevalence of themes based around the Persian War, the invasion of Greece by Philip II of Macedon, and Alexander the Great's conquest of the Persian empire.[34]

Why this emphasis upon these particular phases of classical Greek history? Scholarship has long been aware of the importance of such narratives for preserving Greek identity, by focusing on the glories of the past. But did they hold any resonance for the present? A passage in a contemporary text may offer a clue. When he offers his friend Menemachus, an aspirant politician, advice on how to address the crowd, Plutarch (CE *c.* 40–118) warns him off themes such as 'Marathon, Eurymedon, and Plataea' (sites of famous Greek victories against the Persians: *Political Advice* 814c): mentions of these will only inflame the mob's passions.[35] The imaginative leap from Rome to Persia was not hard to make: the word *satrap*, for example, originally used of Persian viceroys, was routinely adopted for Roman provincial governors.[36] Even the phrase *ho basileus* ('the king'), used by second-century Greeks of the current emperor, echoed the classical Greek

---

[33] Bowie (1974), 170–3; Russell (1983), 106–28; Anderson (1993), 103–19. Kohl (1915) lists all known themes for historical declamations. The most detailed discussion of the topic in modern scholarship is Swain (1996), 92–6; at p. 95, he calculates the relative frequency of historically-based declamations in the contexts of public performance and exercises.

[34] Bowie (1974), 170–2; Russell (1983), 117–19; Swain (1996), 95–6.

[35] See further Jones (1971), 113–14.

[36] Cf. Dio Chrysostom, *Orations* 7.66, 7.93, 47.9, 49.6, 50.6 ('satrap' at 66.12 and 77/8.28, and at Lucian, *Nigrinus* 20, may also refer to Roman governors); Philostratus, *VS* 524. For the Greek terms used of Roman government, see Mason (1974).

means of denoting the Great King of Persia. That Rome could be imagined, however fleetingly or subtly, as a new Persia gives an interesting new inflection to historical declamations. According to Philostratus, specialists in declamation based on Persian themes included Scopelian of Clazomenae (*VS* 519–20) and Ptolemy of Naucratis (*VS* 595).

Turning to Philip II, the most notable feature here is the huge preponderance of imitations of the fourth-century BCE orator Demosthenes, the orator who vainly sought to mobilize the Athenians against expansionist Macedon (particularly in the *Olynthiacs*, the *Philippics*, *On the False Embassy*).[37] Polemo was a great admirer of his: half of his themes recorded by Philostratus are Demosthenic;[38] Philostratus also refers to the 'Demosthenic quality' (*to Dēmosthenikon*) of his thought (*VS* 542).[39] Polemo even set up a statue of him in the Asclepieium of Pergamum.[40] The inscribed base survives, proclaiming that the dedication was the result of a dream. Dreams of literary heroes are not uncommon,[41] but the degree of Polemo's identification with his famous forebear is no less remarkable for that.

Demosthenes' appeal to sophists like Polemo rests partly on his style, muscular yet fluent.[42] The contents of his speeches too, however, surely resonated with the second-century orators. When Dio Chrysostom fled from Domitian's harassment of philosophers, as Philostratus tells it, he took with him two texts: Plato's *Phaedo* and *On the False Embassy* (*VS* 488). The *Phaedo* (which tells the story of Socrates' cheerful death at the hands of the Athenians, and of the immortality of the soul) is an obvious allegory for endurance in the face of state persecution. The choice of *On the False Embassy*, meanwhile, implicitly alleged flattery, corruption, and betrayal at the

---

[37] Swain (1996), 96 calculates that 36% of the identifiable 'historical' declamations in Philostratus have Demosthenic themes.

[38] i.e. 5 out of the 10 recorded at *VS* 538, 542–3. Aelius Aristides was also fond of Demosthenes: cf. fragments 7, 48, 63 Behr.

[39] He is also implicitly linked with Demosthenes at *VS* 539: Herodes is hailed as 'the equal of Demosthenes', to which he replies 'I wish I were the equal of the Phrygian [i.e. Polemo]'.

[40] Habicht (1969), 75 (no. 33) *OSG*, 399 (no. 210). Phrynichus snipes at Polemo's use of Greek on the inscription (*Eclogue* 396 Fischer).

[41] Cf. e.g. Philostratus, *VS* 490 (Dio appears to Favorinus). Comparable, though different, are Lucian's two works entitled *The Dream*: in the one, *paideia* appears to the speaker, encouraging him to find fame abroad; the other is a dream-dialogue between a certain Micyllus and his cock, who turns out to be the reincarnation of Pythagoras. For explicit identifications between 2nd-century authors and classical predecessors (e.g. Arrian as 'the new Xenophon'), see Fein (1994), 120–1; Schmitz (1997), 46–7; 226–7; Whitmarsh (2001), 27.

[42] See Rutherford (1998) for the approbation of Hermogenes and others.

court of the tyrant Domitian, just as Demosthenes had attacked his rival Aeschines on the grounds of complicity with Philip. The story of Demosthenes as proud defender of Greek freedom against foreign tyranny continued to resonate under the empire.

Let us turn finally to the figure of Alexander the Great, an iconic figure for second-century Hellenism.[43] The paradox here is that whereas in the Demosthenes themes the Macedonians (and sometimes Alexander himself: *VS* 538, 596, 620) represent the tyrannical foreign ogre, other speeches represent him as an icon of Hellenism.[44] The fullest example of declamation based around Alexander comes in the shape of Plutarch's pair of speeches *On the Fortune or Virtue of Alexander*. These two texts are clearly performance pieces (even if they are not conventional *meletai*).[45] Plutarch's question as to whether Alexander prospered more through the benevolence of fate or his own intrinsic qualities is presented in the competitive terms of a sophistic *agōn*: he imagines a 'mighty contest between fortune and virtue' (344e) during his life, and now, many years later, a 'discourse supporting Fortune' and 'a rejoinder on behalf of philosophy' (326d). Plutarch argues vigorously that Alexander's success was due to his virtue, and that Fortune was if anything conspicuously hostile to him. Alexander thus emerges as a notably idealized figure (in stark contrast to the more ambivalent treatment in his *Life of Alexander*, and his downright hostile treatment in first-century Roman sources),[46] a hyper-Greek figure.[47] Particularly striking is his recasting of Alexander as a practical philosopher (327e–9d), in line with the privileging of *paideia* (education) in Plutarch's own time: 'a few of us read Plato's *Laws*, but myriads of people have used and continue to

---

[43] Alexandrian themes recur in the second and fourth orations of Dio Chrysostom (as well as in his lost work *On the Virtues of Alexander*: *Suda* s.v. 'Dio son of Pasicrates'), in Plutarch's two speeches *On the Fortune or Virtue of Alexander* (see main text) and *Life of Alexander*, and in Arrian's *Anabasis of Alexander*. Lucian's *Alexander or the False Prophet* is plausibly an inversion of encomiastic portrayals of Alexander (see further pp. 77–8). At the outset, Lucian compares his work to Arrian's life of Tillorobus (or Tilloborus, 2), an otherwise unknown text; Arrian was, of course, most famous for his biography of Alexander (see above ch. 1, 'Education, elitism, and Hellenism').

[44] This ambivalence could already be seen in 4th-century Athens: Isocrates, for example, was strongly supportive of Philip II. See e.g. Whitmarsh (2004a), 162 on the different perceptions of the Macedonians.

[45] Often, but wilfully, attributed to his youth by scholars reluctant to see the mature Plutarch besmirched by sophistry. See e.g. Jones (1971), 67. On the connection between the two Alexander speeches, see Schröder (1991).

[46] Whitmarsh (2002) on Plutarch's *Life*; Fears (1974) on the Roman Stoic tradition, embodied in Lucan and Seneca.

[47] Humbert (1991).

use Alexander's laws' (328e). Under Alexander, the Macedonians are represented as fulfilling the commission set by Isocrates in the fourth century BCE, to unify the world under the civilizing influence of Greek rule.[48]

How does Roman rule measure up to Alexander's civilized empire? Plutarch does not tell us. But he did write an intriguing speech, along the same lines as the Alexander declamations, called *On the Fortune of the Romans*; here, he argues that the Romans owe their dominance primarily to Fortune. We know nothing about the relationship between the two sets of declamations (were they all performed together?), but they surely demand to be read in tandem. At first sight, this would make for a shocking inference: Alexander succeeded through his own qualities, the Romans through chance. There had been, indeed, hostile Greeks who had claimed that the Romans had simply benefited from good luck.[49] Scholars have been unanimous, however, in denying this interpretation, and claiming that Plutarch is actually praising Rome.[50] 'Fortune' (*tykhē*) can mean either random luck or divinely sanctioned providence. Plutarch begins with the former sense (Fortune is accused of being 'a good thing but uncertain', 316c), but redefines it in the course of the essay as a personified, rational, generous, and providential being, looking over the city:[51]

When she approached the Palatine and crossed the Tiber, she seems to have taken off her wings, stepped out of her sandals, and abandoned her untrustworthy and wobbly globe. Thus did she enter Rome to stay, and that is how she is today . . . . (318a)[52]

So for Rome, Fortune means no longer the capriciousness of chance (her fickleness symbolized by the wings, sandals, and globe), but the will of the gods. Rome is the beneficiary of divine favour, not just a series of flukes. To take this text simply as an encomium of Roman might, however, is too hasty. The ending of the text, in particular, pulls the reader up short. 'To Fortune I also ascribe Alexander's death', Plutarch writes, for he was travelling to Rome 'like a shooting star' when he died (326a). What would have happened if Alexander had confronted the Romans? Earlier Greeks had fantasized a Greek

---

[48]   For Isocrates and the civilizing mission of Greek *paideia*, see esp. Usher (1993).

[49]   Cf. Polybius 1.63.9; Dionysius of Halicarnassus, *Roman Antiquities* 1.4.2 (though this passage is surely an imitation of the Polybius passage); Bowersock (1965), 108–10.

[50]   Hamilton (1969), xxiii–xxxiii; Jones (1971), 68; Swain (1989); (1996), 160.

[51]   e.g. 324d ('Fortune saved the city . . . '); 326a ('Fortune's kindness'). See esp. Swain (1989).

[52]   The sentence is finished by the phrase 'as though for a trial', which seems corrupt.

victory in this hypothetical contest,[53] but Plutarch comes to no conclusion: 'I do not think it would have been settled without the spilling of blood', he paraphrases (326c—Homer, *Odyssey* 18.149). The speech ends in suspense. Did Plutarch simply not finish it, as is conventionally understood? Or did he intend to leave the possibilities unresolved in the reader's mind?

It would be misleading to suggest that many historical declamations pitted Greeks against Romans in the way that Plutarch's do. Aelius Aristides' surviving declamations, for example, give away little by way of possible analogies with the present, not even those on the highly fissile subject of Philip (*Orations* 9–10). Similarly, Polemo's two *controversiae*, set in the aftermath of the Marathon conflict, extol the glorious Greek victory over the barbarians, but without hinting at any possible similarities between Persia and Rome. Lesbonax' speeches are a little spicier—the second *Protreptic* expatiates on the Athenians' role as the 'liberators' of Greece, and as defenders against 'slavery' (5–6)—but there is still nothing explicit. My point is not that historical declamations worked consistently, or even regularly, as anti-Roman allegories, but that while the reader enjoys glorious narratives of Greece's military past, the gates to the realm of fantasy are open wide. Words like 'freedom', 'conquest', 'enslavement' are powerful, evocative terms, with a tendency to resist any safe compartmentalization in the ancient past. Sophistry allowed audiences to enjoy stirring militarist rhetoric in the safe setting of the classical world—with the occasional fleeting thrill of approximation between that distant world and the present.

Mythologies

What of non-historical subjects? Sophistic speeches sometimes deploy what we would call mythological subject matter:[54] Aelius Aristides composed an extant speech based around the embassy to Achilles in book 9 of Homer's *Iliad* (*Oration* 16); Dio of Prusa—in addition to his moralizing discussions of the stories of Philoctetes (*Oration* 52),

[53] Cf. Livy 9.18.6–7 for this pastime of the 'most trivial of the Greeks', usually taken to be Timagenes and/or Metrodorus (Bowersock (1965), 109–10; Breitenbach (1969), 156–7; Sordi (1982), 797; disputed by Fears (1974), 129 n. 99). Polybius, perhaps reacting to early versions of such debates, pronounces Roman military success superior to Macedonian (1.2.4–8).

[54] On the use of Homeric material in the period, see Kindstrand (1973). On mythological themes, see generally Anderson (1993), 47–53.

Nessus (60), and Chryseis (61)—composed a sophistical argument that the Trojans won the Trojan War (in part on the grounds that the ancestors of the mighty Romans would not have been beaten by mere Greeks).[55] More common, however, are *suasoriae* (persuasion speeches) and, particularly, *controversiae* (law-court speeches) based around fictitious characters and situations. The *suasoriae* and *controversiae* of the Greek sophists have traditionally been seen as merely playful speeches, lacking any sense of engagement with contemporary reality. Donald Russell notes that they are usually located in an imaginary world subject to laws and politics different from those of the cities of the Greek East. He calls this 'strange but coherent world' Sophistopolis, noting that '[t]hough set vaguely in the past ... it has no precise time or place'.[56] Why did the Greek sophists expend so much energy imagining a political space that looked a little like classical Athens, a little like the contemporary world, but a lot like neither?

There is a sense in which even fictitious declamations, however, were also 'mythological'. Following Roland Barthes' classic analysis of the semiotic value of cultural debris (adverts, posters, strip-tease shows, wrestling, magazine articles), Mary Beard has proposed that the *controversiae* of the first-century Roman orator Seneca the Elder present the city with narratives that are mythical in the Barthesian sense: they convert real-life issues into a culturally-laden mode of communication, investing these issues with ideological form and value, and thus providing a context for society to debate them.[57] These are, she argues, the 'mythologies' that help Romans to explore issues at the heart of contemporary society.

The emphasis in Greek sophistic themes lies upon war and crisis; upon struggles between rich and poor, parents and children, wives and husbands; on issues of rape and marriage; and on suicidal self-condemnation speeches.[58] Can we see these as 'mythologies' in the Barthesian sense? It might be countered that the primary driving force in the choice of theme is the need for a legal or moral complexity, rather than any desire to explore culturally central issues. Lucian's *controversia Tyrannicide*, for example, is based upon a wickedly convoluted

---

[55] Anderson (2000), 152–4; Saïd (2000), 174–86; Jouan (2002). In his *Progymnasmata* (or 'practice pieces'), Hermogenes mentions topics such as a comparison between Heracles and Odysseus, Andromache's words to Hector, Achilles' words to Deidameia, and Achilles' lament over Patroclus (*RG* 2.15–16).

[56] Russell (1983), 21–39, at 38.

[57] Barthes (1972); Beard (1993).

[58] Russell (1983), 21–39.

premise: a man wishes to assassinate the tyrant, but assassinates his son instead; whereupon the tyrant kills himself. The speech represents the man's argument that he deserves to be rewarded for killing the tyrant, even though he was not directly responsible. Another Lucianic *contro-versia*, *Disowned*, treats a disowned son, a medical expert, who cured his father's insanity, and was hence readmitted into the family; he is now protesting that he is being disowned a second time, for refusing to treat his stepmother (whom he has diagnosed as incurable). In both cases, the narrative situation is, at first sight, merely the premise for a sophisticated legal wrangle on the part of the speaker.

Yet these speeches do perform a substantial amount of cultural labour. Let us look a little closer at Lucian's *Tyrannicide* speech. The setting of the speech is, as expected, the hazy world of Sophisto-polis, loosely based upon classical Athens. The tyrant-slaying itself recalls the famous actions of the Athenians Harmodius and Aristogi-ton, who in 514 BCE plotted to kill the tyrant Hippias: despite only killing his younger brother, Hipparchus, they destabilized the tyranny, and Hippias was expelled in 511 BCE. The classical Athenians saw these actions as the inception of their democratic constitution; similarly, Lucian's tyrannicide tells the court, 'I have come here bringing you democracy' (9; cf. 10, 13). Despite the speech's strong association with the classical Athenian past, however, the discourse of tyranny had strong resonances in the second-century present. The historian Nigel Kennell has written that 'the threat of local tyrannies was a real incitement to fear in the Greek cities of the Roman empire, a fear that was not completely without foundation'.[59] Powerful locals could easily brutalize and exploit their fellow-citizens, a phenomenon that was routinely described as tyranny. An excellent case is the trial of Herodes Atticus before Marcus Aurelius, which we discussed above ('Figured speech'): according to Philostratus, the Athenians' complaint was precisely that he was acting like a tyrant (*VS* 559). Dio Chrysostom was similarly accused by his fellow citizens in Prusa (*Oration* 47.23–4). In Kennell's view, tyrannicide speeches such as Lucian's—and there were large numbers of them[60]—were

---

[59] Kennell (1997), 351. For the contemporary relevance of tyrannicide themes, see also Russell (1983), 32–3.

[60] For Philostratus, the Second Sophistic definitively involves characterizations of 'the poor and the rich, excellent men and tyrants' (*VS* 481); Lucian too characterizes his sophis-tic past in terms of 'the accusation of tyrants and the praise of excellent men' (*Double Accu-sation* 32). Sophistic themes based around tyrants are collected and discussed by Russell (1983), 32–3, and esp. Kennell (1997), 351–6.

not simply pleasant diversions; rather, they kept alive the ancient memory of tyrants to serve the ideological needs of the present.

The themes of *Disowned* are less overtly political, but no less culturally central. Quarrels between parents and children are a common source for both declamation and wider literature (particularly tragedy and new comedy).[61] In Lucian's text, the son protests that his father has been aggressive and overbearing towards him: his 'anger', in particular, is a recurrent complaint (1, 3, 8, 9 etc.), closely linked to the psychopathy of which the son has cured him (especially in the closing chapter, 32). As in the tyrannicide speech, Lucian's speaker appeals powerfully to ideological norms contravened by those in power: 'Nature commands fathers to love their children more than she commands children to love their fathers ... you are committing a crime against nature' (18–19). Such assertions are clearly questionable (why *should* fathers love sons more than sons fathers?), but their very questionability is surely the point. The fictitious scenario of the *controversia*, the law-court speech, always dramatizes an implicitly opposing view. *Controversiae* invite audiences to take their own positions on these heavily charged ideological issues, even if they are translated into the distant world of Sophistopolis.

Reading sophistic texts, then, turns out to be a much more challenging enterprise than is often allowed. These are not simply the trivial *jeux* of the idle rich: they are often culturally central works, and the audience are very much engaged in the process of meaning-making. Sophists, as we have seen, were adept in the arts of 'figuring' speech, of the manipulation of personae and narratives to the situation in hand. The subtlety of the sophists—exquisite but elusive—is their greatest legacy; and, indeed, it had a wide impact on contemporary literature, as we shall see in the following chapter.

---

[61] Russell (1983), 31.

V. THE SECOND SOPHISTIC AND IMPERIAL GREEK LITERATURE

This book has focused so far upon the extraordinary popularity of epideictic oratory in the first three centuries of the Roman empire, the 'Second Sophistic' in Philostratus' sense (notwithstanding its distant roots in the fourth century BCE). We have seen that these declamations were performance pieces, and that issues of identity were explored through the observation of the sophist's body; that language and style were heavily theorized, but also highly experimental; and that the interpretation of these ingenious, mobile texts demands considerable resourcefulness and attentiveness. What I want to explore in this final chapter is the points of intersection between these aspects of sophistic literature and the wider literary culture of Roman Greece. I shall focus particularly on two areas, which are central to both oratorical declamation and wider literary culture: 'the self' and exotic narrative.

Writing the self

Let us begin with this modish phrase, 'the self'. It is often claimed that the early Roman empire was a period that saw a new emphasis upon individual persons, and conceived of their primary obligations in terms of a moral relationship to themselves rather than society at large.[1] This is not a proposition that can be properly explored within the limited confines of this book, but its centrality to modern scholarship invites us to consider whether sophistry fed into any culture of self-scrutiny. One of the central issues in chapter 2, on performance culture, was identity: within the traditional expectations of deportment, sophists created for themselves and paraded before others their own unique forms of manly, elite, Greek identity. I want to begin by considering other forms of 'writing the self' in other fields, concentrating particularly on biography, what the Greeks called the *bios*.

The *bios* was not new to Roman Greece.[2] Historiography had always contained biographical elements. Herodotus' and Thucydides'

---

[1] See esp. Veyne (1978); Foucault (1986); Perkins (1995); Edwards (1997); Toohey (2004).

[2] On ancient biography, see esp. Momigliano (1993), whose survey however thins out under the empire; on biography in the Roman empire, Swain and Edwards eds (1997).

Histories feature biographical sections (e.g. what we call book 1 of Herodotus, largely on Croesus); in the following century, Xenophon's *Cyropaedia* was a detailed and sustained account of the life of Cyrus the Great, and Theopompus' *Philippic History*, while infamously adorned with digressions, was organized around the life of one man. Also in the fourth century BCE, Xenophon (*Agesilaus*) and Isocrates (*Evagoras*) produced accounts of the lives of individuals: not, perhaps, what we would call biographies (i.e. full accounts of the lives of the men), but laudatory encomia (Isocrates claims to have inaugurated this genre: *Evagoras* 8). These latter texts stand at the head of twin traditions, both the *bios* or biography and the rhetorical encomium. During the subsequent Hellenistic period, lives of great figures—poets, philosophers, generals, and kings—were composed, often under the influence of Aristotle's Peripatetic school of philosophy: the dominant figures were Aristoxenus of Tarentum (*Lives of Men*, actually fourth century BCE), Antigonus of Carystus (*Lives of the Philosophers*, third century BCE), Hermippus of Smyrna (various works, third century BCE), Satyrus of Callatis on the Black Sea (various, third century BCE), Sotion of Alexandria (*The Succession of the Philosophers*, third century BCE), Polybius (*Philopoemen*, second century BCE), and Didymus (various, first century BCE). A four-page papyrus of Satyrus' *Life of Euripides* represents the only substantial survival from this vast array of Hellenistic biography.[3] The earliest surviving biographies in the conventional sense, meanwhile, are the Latin *Lives of Illustrious Men* of Cornelius Nepos (first century BCE).

Still, it is true to say, with Simon Swain, that '[t]he Greek and Latin literature of the Roman Empire displays a marked biographical trend'. Biography in the imperial period shows not only a marked increase, but also substantial diversification (although, to be sure, the near-total absence of any surviving Hellenistic biography makes it very difficult to determine the extent of this exactly). Even discounting the massive proliferation of biographies of holy men in later antiquity, the first three centuries show a huge range: of (partially or wholly) surviving texts only, we have (in Greek) the *Life of Augustus* of Nicolaus of Damascus,[4] Plutarch's *Lives of the Caesars* and *Parallel Lives*, Lucian's *Demonax, Alexander or the False Prophet*, and *Peregrinus*, Philostratus' *In Honour of Apollonius of Tyana* and *Lives of the Sophists*, the *Lives of the Philosophers* of Diogenes Laertius; (in Latin) Tacitus' *Agricola*,

---

[3] Edited by Arrighetti (1964).
[4] *FGrH* 90 F125–30.

Suetonius' *On Illustrious Men* and *On the Lives of the Caesars*, and the *Historia Augusta* (some of which was, however, composed later).[5] What we see in many of these texts is a (probably new) attentiveness to the inner workings of the psyches of great men (not, apparently, women, in the pagan tradition at any rate), as well as to the details of their private lives.

The historical causes of this phenomenon are no doubt complex, and this is not the place for debate.[6] My interest here lies more narrowly in the cross-fertilization between the simultaneous rapid growth of interest in biography and in epideictic oratory. As we have seen, the earliest 'biographies' (if that is the right word) were encomia, namely Xenophon's *Agesilaus* and Isocrates' *Evagoras*. These remained influential upon the encomiastic tradition under the empire.[7] Menander Rhetor, for example, recommends a technique drawn from the *Evagoras* in his advice on encomia addressed to emperors, and later describes the same text as a 'pure encomium' (372, 419 Russell and Wilson). Imperial encomia continue to contain large sections of biography (however idealized), and standardly trace the subject's progression from birth to death (or the present day), focusing upon his virtues;[8] it is clear, then, that the opportunities for overlap between the two fields are great.

Can we, conversely, trace the impact of epideictic oratory on biography? One example of a work that operates on the cusp between the two is Philostratus' *In Honour of Apollonius of Tyana* (composed probably in the 220s CE). The phrase 'in honour of' (*ta es*) in the title identifies the encomiastic element.[9] In his preface, Philostratus writes that his narrative is 'for the glory (*timē*)' of its subject (1.3); and, indeed, it does include all the standard *topoi* of the speech of praise (ancestry, birth, nature, physical being, education, deeds, virtues, death).[10] The text is not, however, a simple encomium: it borrows elements

---

[5] For a fuller survey of imperial biography, see Swain (1997), 22–37.

[6] In the most analysis, this explosion of interest in the biographical is attributed to changes in social and political structures, in particular a widening gap between elite and mass, coupled with a greater emphasis upon state surveillance and disciplining (through law, the military, and civic institutions): see Swain (1997), building on Veyne (1978) and Foucault (1986).

[7] On which see esp. Pernot (1993).

[8] Pernot (1993), 1.143–78.

[9] See LSJ s.v. εἰς IV.1.b., (mis)quoting Philostratus' title. For recent bibliography on this text, see esp. Bowie (1978); Anderson (1986), 121–239; Koskenniemi (1991); Bowie (1994); Flintermann (1995); Swain (1996), 381–95, (1999); Elsner (1997), Billault (2000), 105–26. On the authorship of this text, see ch. 2 n. 10.

[10] For which see Pernot (1993), 1.156–78.

from the traditions of biography, paradoxography, and the novel too,[11] forging a new generic combination that would become influential on the later form of hagiography (or 'saint's life').[12] Philostratus' innovation was to produce a sophisticated, full-scale *bios* of a man who was also divine, a *theios anēr*: for this purpose, he created a new form of biography that purloined elements from different genres. The author represents his sage's amazing, exceptional power by ransacking the cultural repertoire for the appropriate comparisons, language, and genre through which to speak of him—and ostentatiously failing.[13] Is he a god? Or a mortal hero? Or, indeed, a fraud?[14] Before his birth, the narrator tells us, Apollonius' mother saw an apparition: Proteus, the famous shape-shifting god, told her that the child she would bear was in fact he (1.4). Proteus, the narrator tells us, was 'multiform (*poikilos*), different at different times, and impossible to catch'. This passage represents a clear signal as to the generic slipperiness of subject and author alike.[15]

Encomium was not the only epideictic genre to feed into biography. Lucian's satirical *Alexander or the False Prophet* (written probably in the 180s) is a brilliant subversion of the encomiastic biography, based around the epideictic *psogos* or speech of reproach (which ancient theorists considered to be the inverse of the encomium).[16] Lucian's narrator begins by addressing a certain Celsus, who has encouraged him to write the 'life' (*bios*) of Alexander of Abonoteichus, an upstart prophet from Paphlagonia; this, the narrator continues, has proven 'no less a task than writing down the deeds of Alexander the son of Philip: for the one's wickedness matches the other's virtue' (1). Lucian's biography will be a malevolent doublet of the familiar lives

[11] For novelistic influences, see Bowie (1978), 1663–7, (1994); Billault (1991).

[12] Cox (1983).

[13] On the ambivalence of the 'divine man' in later antiquity, see Cox (1983). Bieler (1935–6) is still fundamental.

[14] Apollonius' divinity is alluded to at 2.40, 5.36, 7.38, 8.15. He is also linked with mortal heroes, Achilles (3.19; 4.11–12; 4.16) and Alexander (2.9–10; 2.20; 2.24; 2.33; 2.42–3; 3.53). Apollonius is frequently accused of being a *goēs* ('wizard'/'quack'), and the narrator's denials are not always convincing: e.g. at 7.34, where he claims to Domitian that he cannot be a *goēs* because a *goēs* would magically escape from prison ... before magically escaping from prison (7.38)! On Apollonius' trickiness, see esp. Anderson (1986), 121–53.

[15] The author of the *Lives of the Sophists* would have known, too, that sophists were often compared to Proteus: see ch. 1 n. 60.

[16] Pernot (1993), 1.481–90, with 486 on the *Alexander*; also Branham (1989), 190–6, 209. *On the Passing of Peregrinus* is a comparable text, but less biographical in its structure. On the *Alexander*, see Jones (1986), 133–48; Branham (1989), 181–210; Clay (1992); Victor (1997).

of Alexander composed by Plutarch, Arrian, and others. Like *In Honour of Apollonius of Tyana*, the *Alexander* contains all the elements a speech of praise should have (ancestry, birth, nature, physical being, education,[17] deeds, 'virtues', death)—in this case, however, serving the defamation rather than the exaltation of the poor would-be holy man.

The best-known and most sophisticated of imperial biographers, Plutarch (CE *c.* 40–118), avoids any simple, schematic division of his subjects into the praiseworthy and the execrable in his *Parallel Lives* and *Lives of the Emperors* (of which only *Galba* and *Otho* survive).[18] It is of course true that moralism is his central concern, and some of his programmatic statements imply that his subjects will be defined according to their virtues (or in one case, vices).[19] The subject's actions, Plutarch writes at one point, are the 'impression of his character', the 'signs of his soul' (*Alexander* 1.2–3): these are phrases that recur in encomiastic contexts.[20] As a recent commentator has observed, however, a 'number of factors stand in the way of an approach to the *Parallel Lives* which looks for the kind of easily extractable moral lessons that Plutarch seems to promise': the narratives are complex, the evaluation of figures ambivalent, and the authorial guidance intermittent at best.[21] Plutarch's *Lives* are not written for straightforward praise or blame, like the more rhetorically influenced biographies we have already discussed: this material is tough, challenging, and philosophically informed.

Plutarch was not immune to the influence of sophistry. As we saw in the previous chapter, he was himself an accomplished sophist. In addition to the declamations on fortune and virtue, he also composed a sophistic piece asking whether Athens could claim more glory for its military or its cultural exploits. His conclusion—that the military exploits are more impressive—mirrors the preoccupations of both the historical declamations of the Second Sophistic (see chapter 4) and the author's own *Parallel Lives*, which focus exclusively upon men of politics and war.[22] Again like the sophists' themes, the Greek

---

[17] Indeed, at the hands (and more) of an acolyte of Apollonius of Tyana (5).

[18] Among the huge number of recent works on Plutarch's *Lives*, particularly notable are: Russell (1972), 100–42; Scardigli ed. (1995); Swain (1996), 137–61; Duff (1999); Pelling (2002).

[19] Esp. *Pericles* 1.4, 2.1–4 (virtue); *Aemilius Paulus* 1.1–3 (virtue); *Demetrius* 1.3–6 (vice). On these passages, see esp. Duff (1999), 30–49.

[20] Menander Rhetor 372.5 Russell and Wilson; Julian, *Oration* 1.4d.

[21] Duff (1999), 54–5. On moral complexity in the *Lives*, see also Pelling (1995).

[22] Solon and Demosthenes, who receive lives, were of course authors *as well as* politicians.

subjects of Plutarch's *Lives* all derive from the period before the Roman conquest: the latest is Philopoimen, who fought against the invading army of Flamininus (the subject of the paired Roman *Life*). It would be misleading, however, to suggest an exact correspondence: Plutarch is much more catholic in his subjects, in terms of both geography (including figures such as Dio of Sicily and Pyrrhus of Epirus) and history (running down to the early second century BCE). The *Lives*, composed to stimulate rigorous reflection, situate themselves far from the nascent world of the Second Sophistic.

Autobiographies and apologetics

If biography is a difficult genre to pin down, autobiography is all the more so.[23] Unlike with *bios* ('life', hence 'biography'), no ancient word exists for autobiography; and, relatedly, there is no sharply defined concept of the genre. There are, of course, all kinds of texts that have substantial amounts of personal narrative in them, from Plato's seventh *Letter* and Xenophon's *Anabasis*, through the now-lost personal records of Hellenistic courtiers, through the *Achievements* (*Res Gestae*) of Augustus and other emperors, to Marcus Aurelius' *Meditations* and Saint Augustine's *Confessions*. It is practically meaningless, however, to ask whether or not such texts count as autobiography, a genre that is an entirely modern construct.

A more interesting question to ask is whether or not the intense focus on the cultivation and presentation of personal identity that we see in the Second Sophistic (see chapter 2) interlaced with a more general interest in narratives about the author's own person (which I shall continue to call 'autobiography', to avoid cumbersome circumlocution). We saw above how closely biography relates to epideictic encomium. Analogously, it is notable how many examples of what modern scholars call 'autobiography' are really what ancient theorists would have called rhetorical *apologiai* ('defence-speeches'). Socrates' defence-speech in court, whether mediated through Plato's or Xenophon's version, soon became an autobiographical classic; it was already imitated by the fourth-century orators Isocrates (*Antidosis*) and Lycurgus (who wrote perhaps two *Apologies*).[24]

---

[23] For surveys, see Misch (1950); Baslez, Hoffmann and Pernot eds (1993). There is also valuable material in Momigliano (1993).
[24] II–III Durrbach.

With the advent of the empire, there seems to have been a resurgence of interest in the apology, both as a general type and as an evocation of the Socratic hypotext (once again, the near-total obliteration of Hellenistic prose makes it difficult to judge the extent of this phenomenon). Writing around the time of Augustus (for whom, as we saw above, he composed a *bios*), Nicolaus of Damascus composed an autobiography, *On his Own Life and Upbringing*.[25] Nicolaus appears to have been attacked on the grounds of financial irregularity: in the autobiography, he 'produced an *apologia* on the question of money', and extolled his own moral virtue (*FGrH* 90 F138).

Flavius Josephus, who knew Nicolaus' other work well enough to use it in his *Jewish Antiquities*, also composed an autobiography, which has come down to us under the title of *The Life (bios) of Josephus* (probably CE *c.* 100). This is the earliest fully extant work approximating to what we would call autobiography to come down to us from before late antiquity. Once again, however, it is fundamentally an apologetic work. Though like other *bioi* it contains an account of the author's ancestry, birth, and education, its primary focus is upon defending the author from the allegations made in a history of the Jewish War produced by a rival historian, Justus of Tiberias. This is made explicit in a digression (336–67), where, using emphatically legalistic language, he describes himself as 'compelled to produce an *apologia*, because false testimony has been brought against me'.[26]

In the second century, the close link between autobiography and *apologia* intensified. Writing in Latin (but strongly attuned to the currents of Greek sophistry, as recent scholars have observed), Apuleius of Madaura in north Africa (*c.* 123–70) produced his quasi-Socratic *Apology* on the charge of witchcraft.[27] The master of the autobiographical *apologia*, however, was the satirist Lucian. In three separate works, he responds apologetically to supposed accusations over a preceding work.[28] In *Defence of 'Portraits'*, 'Lycinus' (a veiled *nom de clef*, for 'Lucian') offers an *apologia* (15) against the 'accusation' (15) of gratuitously flattering Panthea in the *Portraits*; in the *Apology*, he provides an *apologia* (3, 4, 8, 11, 15) against the 'accusation' (3, 4, 5, 6, 8, 11) of hypocrisy, in the light of his views expressed

---

[25] *FGrH* 90 F131–9.

[26] The question of precisely what accusations he is defending himself against, and why, is more complex: see recently Hadas-Lebel (1993), 128–30. Josephus' best-known apologetic work is *Against Apion*, a defence of the Jews against gentile prejudice.

[27] See esp. Harrison (2000), 39–88, with 42–7 on the rhetorical background.

[28] See further Whitmarsh (2001), 291–2.

in *On Salaried Posts* about Greek intellectuals in Roman service; in the dialogue *The Fisherman*, 'Parrhesiades' (another *nom de clef* for the satirist) presents an *apologia* (15, 28), in a forensic setting, before the revivified philosophers who think they have been humiliated in *The Sale of Lives*. The dialogue *The Double Accusation*, meanwhile, centres around charges brought against 'the Syrian' by Rhetoric and Dialogue that he has debased both: Lucian's *apologia* (34) carries the day. These texts are not 'autobiographical' in the sense of constructing a coherent, continuous narrative; but they do make deliberate and knowing use of the genre of the *apologia* to construct an identity for the author as a culturally and generically transgressive figure.[29]

Self-description and self-praise

The link between the rhetorical form of the *apologia* and the autobiography appears to have been strong and enduring. It would be naïve, though, to conclude on this basis that the autobiographies in question are simply defensive. The rhetorical apology was also a form of self-promotion. At one level, the ever-present intertextual relationship with the prestigious precedent of Socrates guarantees that any apology will also constitute a claim for a certain cultural importance. Greek writers under the empire had further sophisticated resources to hand, however.

Early imperial rhetorical theory was fascinated by the problem of *periautologia*, or 'how to talk about oneself'.[30] Plutarch's essay *On Praising Oneself without Causing Envy* is the most extended and important account. How can one 'speak about oneself as though one were important or powerful' (539a) without inspiring resentment? 'First and foremost', Plutarch writes, 'you can praise yourself without causing offence if you do this when you are delivering an apology, in response either to slander or to an accusation' (540c). In Plutarch's eyes, then, the apology presented a rare opportunity to praise oneself without fear of redress.

It may be, then, that the apologetic framing of the autobiographies of Nicolaus and Josephus is designed primarily to divert the charge

---

[29] On Lucian's self-fashioning through texts such as this, see Saïd (1993); Dubel (1994).

[30] Rutherford (1995), 199–201. Add Alexander's *On the Difference between Praise and Encomium* = *RG* 3.2–4.

of *periautologia*, of 'talking about oneself': both texts are, indeed, otherwise far from reticent in their self-praise. Aelius Aristides' *Concerning a Remark in Passing* (28) is an ingenious variation on this theme.[31] Aristides claims to have been criticized for injecting into a speech to Athena some words of self-congratulation. *Concerning a Remark in Passing* defends him on this charge ... while of course taking the chance to praise himself all the more! Even the accusation, as reported by Aristides, is really a compliment: that he praised himself when 'everyone knows how much better my [i.e. Aristides'] speeches are' (2). The speech as a whole, however, becomes a masterful synopsis of literary examples of *periautologia*, from Homer to Demosthenes.

Lucian too, as we have seen, speaks about himself in defence. In this case, matters are more complex. Lucian is at one level one of antiquity's most periautological figures, to the extent that entire biographies have been reconstructed from his transmitted texts alone.[32] As we have seen above, his apologetic speeches give the impression of a controversial author, at the heart of a dynamic but disputatious literary society. In texts like *Alexander or the False Prophet*, *Demonax* and *Nigrinus*, we see an intellectually committed figure, well connected to important philosophical movers of the day. *On the Syrian Goddess*, meanwhile (if it is genuinely Lucianic) represents him as a Syrian and once-devotee of the cult of Atargatis in Hierapolis. Finally, one of his prologue speeches, transmitted under the title *The Dream or Lucian's Life* (where 'life' translates *bios*), narrates a dream the author claims to have had when he was young: two apparitions, Education (*paideia*) and Craft (*technē*) appeared before him, vying for his favour, the one offering life-changing riches, and the other family continuity.[33] As a cute account of the unremarkable life of a provincial hick, this speech presents an obvious starting point for would-be biographers.

And yet, as recent scholarship has emphasized, Lucian's 'I' is devious and elusive.[34] In the dialogues, the satirical figure is never styled 'Lucian': the names that recur are 'Lycinus', 'Parrhesiades' ('free-speaker'), 'Momus' ('blame'), 'Tychiades' ('Man of fortune').[35] Even

---

[31] See Rutherford (1995) on this text.

[32] Most fully by Schwartz (1965).

[33] See most recently Whitmarsh (2001), 122–4; Goldhill (2002b), 67–9.

[34] Saïd (1993); Dubel (1994); Whitmarsh (2001), 248–53; Goldhill (2002b), 67–82.

[35] The exception is the *False Sophist*, where the name 'Lucian' is given to one of the interlocutors (but it is never used in the text proper, and may be an interpolation).

in the non-dialogic texts, the name is only rarely disclosed.[36] The various views that his narrator espouses are notoriously inconsistent. Indeed, the very question of where the author's 'true' identity lies seems to entangle us in a web of complex but playful Lucianisms: after all, this is the same person who wrote, in a text entitled *True Histories*, that 'the one true thing I shall write is that I am lying' (1.4). Lucian teases his readers with the possibility of a real author underneath, while larding his texts self-consciously with tall stories. It is hard not to agree with a commentator who writes that 'despite the omnipresence of the "I", Lucian's work is ... the inverse of autobiography'.[37]

As we have seen, though, and as the same commentator proceeds to note, autobiography 'proper' cannot avoid rhetorical self-promotion. In the highly sophisticated, self-aware literary culture that flourished alongside the Second Sophistic, writing or speaking about oneself was seen as a bid for status, repute, and 'cultural capital'. Like the sophists (and indeed all the figures discussed in this section—Plutarch, Aristides, and Lucian—had been or were sophists), albeit through the different medium of the literary text, autobiographers were seeking to promote themselves in the world through the construction of a publicly orientated persona.

The suffering self

It would be misleading, however, to suggest that all early imperial autobiographies were built around naked self-promotion, or dizzying Lucianic deconstructions of that process. The *Sacred Discourses* of Aelius Aristides, written in the 170s (but describing events of the last 30 years), are often cited as an example of ancient autobiography at its most introspective and intense.[38] Five of these extraordinary texts survive (as *Orations* 47–51), as well as a brief fragment of a sixth (*Oration* 52). Their subject is Aristides' recurrent painful illness, and particularly the god Asclepius' interventions to heal him. Asclepius manifested himself regularly to Aristides in dreams, giving

---

[36] Nigrinus 1; *True Histories* 2.28; *The Dream or Lucian's Life* (title); *Alexander or the False Prophet* 55; *On the Death of Peregrinus* 1; *Epigram* 1 Macleod. See further Whitmarsh (2001), 253.

[37] Saïd (1993), 270 (my translation).

[38] Misch (1950), 2.495–510 (though denying that this is true autobiography); Quet (1993), 213–16. See further Behr (1968); Pearcy (1988); Perkins (1995), 173–89; Swain (1996), 260–74.

instructions, which usually turn out to involve fasting, vomiting, and/ or not bathing. The central theme of the texts is thus Aristides' ongoing devotion to the god, and his struggles to interpret the dream-signs.

Why did Aristides write these texts? The simplistic explanation that he was a hypochondriac will not do:[39] these texts manifest a sense of pride, if anything, not anxiety. A better point of departure is presented by Judith Perkins, who focuses not on Aristides' mental state (ultimately inscrutable, especially in the anachronistic terms of modern psychology), but on the representation of bodily suffering in the *Sacred Discourses*.[40] What is interesting about these texts is the set of claims they make about Aristides' fortitude and divine favour. The author's body, and the extreme demands made upon it, become the central focus of interest: 'The state of my stomach, palate, whole head, and entire body became such that I came to the limit: I was prevented from taking any food, whatever I approached immediately turned rotten, I could not breathe, my power had been removed' (*Oration* 47.69). For Perkins, this emphasis on pain can be paralleled across a wide range of contemporary texts, including the Christian martyr acts, and testifies to an increasing desire to represent the body as the primary site of ideological and cultural conflict.[41]

What this approach also points up, however, is a paradox. The representation of pain becomes a way of laying claim to true, authentic experience: this is the verbal equivalent of showing one's scars, by way of saying 'I've *been* there'. Aristides is not playing the sophist here, but the devotee: 'sacred discourses' (*hieroi logoi*) are, conventionally, the texts that one leaves behind inscribed at a cult-site as personal testimony to the god's power.[42] And yet it is hard to forget that Aristides was indeed an orator, and among the most brilliant and successful. Do the *Sacred Discourses*, then, represent 'genuine' theological devotion, or are they a calculated attempt to raise the orator's status by capitalizing on his notorious[43] ill health?

Certainly, Aristides is conscious of his public. He represents himself as divulging deep secrets to them: 'I want to reveal . . .' (47.4); 'But now

[39] Dodds (1965), 39–45, ably dismissed by Swain (1996), 106–9.
[40] Perkins (1995), 173–89.
[41] See also the classic discussion of Brown (1989).
[42] Quet (1993), 236–9.
[43] Philostratus, *VS* 581. In a passage of his commentary on Plato's *Timaeus*, transmitted in Arabic, Galen also alludes to Aristides' health problems; the passage is translated at Behr (1968), 162.

I wish to reveal to you ...' (48.2). This process of 'revelation' mimics the process whereby the god 'reveals' his advice to Aristides himself (48.75, 51.67): the god's favourite arrogates to himself a prominent role in the chain of dissemination (Asclepius > Aristides > the world). At one point in a separate address to Asclepius, he even refers to himself as the 'actor' (*hupokritēs*) of the god's words (*Oration* 42.12),[44] just as a sophist would act out the role of a Demosthenes or Alexander in a declamatory *meletē*. What is more, for all their apparent disorder (mimicking the chaos of a dream-world), the *Sacred Discourses* are extremely sophisticated at the level of structure and expression.[45]

Whether it would be right to conclude on this basis that this 'autobiography' is another case of sophistic self-promotion, however, is a moot point. The point is, surely, that the question is wrongly phrased. All autobiography is caught between the revelation of intimate secrets and the fashioning of a public persona.[46] The case of Aelius Aristides, the world-famous sophistic declaimer who thought fit to commit to print his intimate communion with Asclepius, is simply a particularly well-sharpened example of the phenomenon. It is in particular our awareness that Aristides was a practising orator (an identity, moreover, that he proclaims repeatedly within the *Sacred Discourses*) that injects the uncertainty into our interpretation of the text. Sophistry, as we have seen repeatedly throughout this book, teaches audiences to be sceptical and critical, particularly about claims to authoritative speech.

Aristides instantiates not so much a new stage in this history of the self as a new way of conceiving of the relationship between inner self and outer expression. The level of intimate detail in the *Sacred Discourses* is matched only by their author's (shocking, to modern eyes) willingness to divulge it: 'now I wish to reveal to you the matter of my belly' (48.2). It is possible that the epideictic culture that Aristides inhabited, with all of its focus upon external self-presentation, actually helped to fire the second century's fascination with inwardness. Certainly the *Sacred Discourses* gain much of their force from the powerful tension between the private world of Aristides' dreams and sicknesses, and the subtle brilliance of its exposition in language.

---

[44]   The text is uncertain, but there is no reason to doubt the word *hupokritēs*.
[45]   Pearcy (1988); Whitmarsh (2004f).
[46]   See e.g. Sturrock (1993).

Novel directions

The history of the self is one area where an awareness of the parallel phenomenon of the Second Sophistic can make a difference. I turn now to another field, that of the Greek novel. 'The Greek novel' is a modern phrase, designating a group of five texts composed in the first four centuries CE. On the conventional dating (which remains controversial), Chariton's *Chaereas and Callirhoe* and the *Ephesian Story* of Xenophon of Ephesus belong in the first century CE, Achilles Tatius' *Leucippe and Clitophon* and Longus' *Daphnis and Chloe* in the second, and Heliodorus' *Ethiopian Story* in the fourth.[47] All five texts are fictional (that is to say, they use invented plots and characters—notwithstanding the appearance of the historical general Hermocrates in Chariton), are set more or less specifically in the classical past, and focus on the trials and separations of young, heterosexual lovers of roughly equal age.[48] It is probably misguided to speak of the novel as 'invented' during the early imperial period (there were precedents of sorts during the Hellenistic period, though as ever the loss of most prose from that period makes it impossible to judge with confidence), but it is certainly the most distinctive literary product of the age; and, as we shall see below, there are strong claims to innovation pressed by the novelists themselves.

What do these novels have to do with the Second Sophistic? A good place to start is an observation made by the founder of modern studies of the Greek novel (and, indeed, the Second Sophistic), Erwin Rohde: sophistic declamations (particularly *controversiae*) and novels alike make use of fictional scenarios, often with erotic or sentimental themes.[49] Both genres required artful narrative skills: 'narration' (*diēgēsis*) was a central part of declamation.[50] It is even possible that some of the novelists were practising sophists. Lollianus, the author

---

[47] On the dating, see most recently Bowie (2002b) (on the early novels). Heliodorus is sometimes placed in the third century (see e.g. Swain (1996), 423–4), but there is no strong evidence.

[48] For orientation on the immense bibliography, see Bowie and Harrison eds (1993); more recent works of a general nature include Swain ed. (1999); Schmeling ed. (2003). The novels are also frequently discussed in terms of the supposed 'invention of the self' (see above), in particular for their focus on sexual ethics and marriage. See esp. Konstan (1994); Cooper (1996); Goldhill (1995).

[49] Rohde (1914), 361–87. Russell (1983), 38 modifies this view, claiming that rather than the declamations inspiring the novels, 'both are expressions of a common culture'. On the connections between the novel and epideictic oratory, see also Reardon (1974); Cassin (1986).

[50] Anderson (1993), 156–70.

of a now fragmentary *Phoenician Tale* (which is fictional and exciting, though not obviously a heterosexual romance), may be the prestigious sophist Publius Hordeonius Lollianus recorded in Philostratus (*VS* 526–7).[51] Some scholars believe that Heliodorus, the author of the *Ethiopian Story*, may have been Philostratus' sophist 'Heliodorus the Arab' (*VS* 625–7).[52] Lucian, finally, was accomplished at both declamatory rhetoric and fiction, as is shown by a number of his works: the *True Stories*, the *Lover of Lies* and *Toxaris* are not novels as we understand them, but they are certainly sophisticated narrative inventions.[53]

There is a certain limited crossover at the level of narrative content, too. Two of the novels (Chariton's *Chaereas and Callirhoe* and Heliodorus' *Ethiopian Story*) are set in specific historical times, but the others are located in a historically hazy world that is remarkably close to what Donald Russell calls 'Sophistopolis':[54] a world of assemblies and mass juries (unlike the Roman present), but also governed oligarchically by the 'best' (as contemporary cities indeed were). As well as adulterers and frustrated lovers, malevolent pirates figure prominently in novels and declamations.[55] It is possible that these pirates reflect contemporary reality (although the heyday of Mediterranean piracy was earlier, in the early first century BCE),[56] but more likely that they represent more vague archaizing (pirates, after all, appear already in the *Odyssey* and the second *Homeric Hymn to Dionysus*).

So far we have identified some broad similarities between the genres, but nothing that is likely to convince readers that they do more than reflect the shared preoccupations of their classes. Yet there is, I think, a closer connection than this. As we saw in chapter 2 ('Norm and deviance'), the competitive structure of sophistic performance demanded a certain investment in innovation, what the Greeks called *to kainon*—counterbalanced, of course, against the expectation of traditional features. Sophists thus frequently (as we saw) lay claim to the 'novelty' of their work. The novel presents itself as comparably 'novel' (even though the pun does not work in Greek). From rhetoric it borrows the language of the paradoxical, the exciting, the

[51]   For a balanced view, see Stephens and Winkler (1995), 316–18; see also *OSG* 327–30 on this sophist. *The Phoenician Story* is well discussed by Winkler (1980).

[52]   Swain (1996), 423–4.

[53]   Ch. 4 n. 28.

[54]   See ch. 4, 'Mythologies'.

[55]   On declamatory pirates, see Russell (1983), 26.

[56]   The *boukoloi* or 'bandits' of Lollianus, Achilles Tatius 3–4 and Heliodorus 1–2, for example, are certainly attested in contemporary society: see Cassius Dio 71.4, and further Winkler (1980).

unexpected.[57] Chariton writes, programmatically, at the start of his text that 'Eros rejoices in paradoxical (*paradoxois*) triumphs' (1.1.4); and elsewhere, similarly, Fortune is described as 'enjoying innovation' (*philokainos*, 4.4.2; cf. 6.8.1, 8.3.6). These self-referential moments mark the novel as revelling in its capacity to surprise the reader, but also as a self-consciously 'new' product in the literary canon.[58]

To illustrate the close fit between sophistic and novelistic claims to innovation, let us compare a passage from Achilles Tatius and a passage from Polemo. In the first, the hero, Clitophon, describes a trap whereby the bandits flood a causeway full of soldiers:

A novel (*kaina*) kind of ill fortune, this: such a terrible shipwreck, with not a ship in sight. Two extraordinary (*paraloga*) novelties (*kaina*): an infantry-battle in the water, and a shipwreck on land! (*Leucippe and Clitophon* 4.14.7–8)

In Polemo's declamation (the first of a pair of *controversiae*), the father of Cynegirus (who died at the battle of Marathon, 490 BCE) claims that his son died more valiantly than Callimachus, and he (the father) should thus deliver the funeral speech. Cynegirus famously held on to one of the Persian ships, and continued to fight after his hand had been amputated:

Now for the first time people saw a sea-battle on land, now for the first time people saw a battle between a man and a ship, now for the first time they saw a right hand confront a prow, now they saw at the same time a hand being cut off, and a ship brought in hand.[59] (A.36)

The parallels in the structure of both paradoxes are evident. It is not simply for cheap thrills, however, that the novels purloin such set pieces from the orators. It is central to their ambitions as literary works that they continue to surprise and challenge their readers. A passage in Plutarch's *How a Young Man Should Listen to Poetry* exemplifies the point: 'Changes in narrative direction furnish stories with an empathetic, surprising (*paralogon*) and unexpected quality; this is what

---

[57] This is particularly prominent in Chariton and Achilles Tatius. Paradoxes in Chariton: 2.8.3, 3.2.7, 3.3.2, 3.3.13, 3.4.1, 4.1.2, 5.8.2, 8.1.2, 8.1.9, 8.6.10. Paradoxes in Achilles: 2.18.6; 4.4.1; 6.2.3 (*paradoxos*); 4.14.5; 4.14.8; 5.1.6; 5.23.5; 6.2.8; 6.4.3 (*paralogos*); 'novel' (*kainos*, listing only the uses meaning 'of a novel kind') phenomena in Achilles: 1.9.5; 2.14.4; 3.3.3; 3.16.4; 4.4.6; 4.7.15; 4.12.1; 4.14.8 (*bis*); 5.1.6; 5.14.4; 6.7.3; 6.21.2. See further Anderson (1993), 163–5.

[58] Whitmarsh (2001), 78–87. The passages from Achilles and Polemo cited below are also compared at Whitmarsh (2001), 79.

[59] *kratoumenēn* is a pun: it could mean either 'held' or 'conquered'. The paradoxical confusion of land and sea can also be found in the second fragment of Hadrian of Tyre, printed at Hinck (1876), 45–6.

generates the maximum shock and pleasure' (25d). The allegiance with competitive sophistry, the literary movement most committed to inventiveness, is thus strategic and significant.

'Eros', claims Achilles Tatius' narrator, 'is a resourceful, improvising sophist, who can turn any place into a temple for his mysteries' (5.27.4).[60] This is Clitophon's explanation for why he consents to have sex with Melite in a prison cell; but like all such sententious sayings concerning Eros and Fortune (the deified abstractions who are held to govern the plots of the novels), it also works at a self-referential level. The god of the Greek novel is indeed an improvising sophist. The novel repeatedly takes traditional material and transforms it into something invigorating and new.

I began this book by narrowing down the definition of the Second Sophistic to the sophistic movement described by Philostratus. What I hope to have shown in this chapter is that that movement, for all that it deserves to be analysed in detail and on its own terms, impacted heavily on the wider literary culture of Roman Greece. Indeed, the two areas with which cultural and literary historians have most concerned themselves in recent years, namely the Greek novel and the supposed intensification of interest in 'the self', were themselves partially impelled by epideictic oratory. The Second Sophistic deserves its central role not just in the narrow history of rhetoric, but in the cultural history of imperial Greece as a whole.

---

[60] Compare 1.10, 'Eros is a self-taught sophist'. The allusion in both cases is to Plato, *Symposium* 203d; cf. Xenophon, *Education of Cyrus* 6.1.41.

BIBLIOGRAPHY

1. Abbreviations

DK = H. Diels and W. Kranz, *Die Fragmente der Vorsokratiker*[6] (Berlin, 1951–2).

EG = G. Kaibel, *Epigrammata Graeca ex lapidibus conlecta* (Berlin, 1878).

FGrH = F. Jacoby, *Die Fragmente der griechischen Historiker* (Berlin and Leiden, 1923–).

IG = *Inscriptiones Graecae*, 2nd ed. (Berlin, 1924–).

KA = R. Kassel and C. Austin eds., *Poetae Comici Graeci* (Berlin, 1983–).

LSJ = H.G. Liddell, R. Scott et al., *A Greek-English Lexicon*, 9th edn. (Oxford, 1996).

OSG = B. Puech, *Orateurs et sophists grecs dans les inscriptions d'époque impériale* (Paris, 2002).

P. Hibeh = Hibeh Papyrus.

P. Berol. = Berlin Papyrus.

RG = L. Spengel ed., *Rhetores Graeci*, 3 vols. (Leipzig, 1856).

UR = H. Usener and L. Radermacher eds., *Dionysius Halicarnaseus Quae extant*, vol. 6 (Leipzig, 1965).

VS = Philostratus, *Lives of the Sophists*.

Abbreviations for journals follow those in *Année Philologique*, with some obvious anglicizations (*AJP* for *AJPh*, etc.)

2. List of Works Cited

Aalders, G.J.D. (1982): *Plutarch's Political Thought* (Amsterdam).

Ahl, F. (1984): 'The Art of Safe Criticism in Greece and Rome', *AJP* 105, 174–208.

Alcock, S.E. (1993): *Graecia capta: The Landscapes of Roman Greece* (Cambridge).

—— (1994): 'Nero at Play? The Emperor's Grecian Odyssey', in J. Elsner and J. Masters eds., *Reflections of Nero: Culture, History, and Representation* (London), 98–111.

—— (2001): 'The Peculiar Book IV and the Problem of the Messenian Past', in S.E. Alcock, J.F. Cherry, and J. Elsner eds., *Pausanias: Travel and Memory in Roman Greece* (New York), 142–53.

Ameling, W. (1983): *Herodes Atticus*, 2 vols. (Hildesheim).

Anderson, G. (1976): 'Some Alleged Relationships in Lucian's Opuscula', *AJP* 97, 262–75.

—— (1986): *Philostratus: Biography and Belles-lettres in the Third Century AD* (Beckenham).

—— (1990): 'The Second Sophistic: Some Problems of Perspective', in Russell ed. (1990), 91–110.

—— (1993): *The Second Sophistic: A Cultural Phenomenon in the Roman Empire* (London).

—— (1994): *Sage, Saint and Sophist: Holy Men and their Associates in the Early Roman Empire* (London).

—— (2000): 'Some Uses of Storytelling in Dio', in S. Swain ed., *Dio Chrysostom: Politics, Letters, and Philosophy* (Oxford), 143–60.

Arrighetti, G. (1964): *Satiro*, Vita di Euripide (Pisa).

Avotins, I. (1975): 'The Holders of the Chairs of Rhetoric at Athens', *HSCP* 79, 313–24.

—— (1978): 'The Date and Recipient of the *Vitae Sophistarum* of Philostratus', *Hermes* 106, 242–7.

Baldwin, B. (1975): *Studies in Aulus Gellius* (Lawrence, KA).

Barthes, R. (1972): *Mythologies*, trans. Annette Lavers (London).

Barton, T.S. (1994): *Power and Knowledge: Astrology, Physiognomics, and Medicine under the Roman Empire* (Ann Arbor).

Bartsch, S. (1994): *Actors in the Audience: Theatricality and Double-speak from Nero to Hadrian* (Cambridge, MA).

Baslez, M.-F, Hoffmann, P., and Pernot, L., eds. (1993): *L'invention de l'autobiographie d'Hésiode à Saint Augustine: actes du deuxième colloque de l'Équipe de recherche sur l'hellénisme post-classique* (Paris).

Beard, M. (1993): 'Looking (Harder) for Roman Myth: Dumézil, Declamation and the Problems of Definition', in F. Graf ed., *Mythos in mythenloser Gesellschaft: das Paradigma Roms* (Stuttgart), 44–64.

Behr, C.A. (1968): *Aelius Aristides and the Sacred Tales* (Amsterdam).

Bieler, L. (1935–6): $\Theta EIO\Sigma$ $ANHP$: das Bild des 'göttlichen Menschen' in Spätantike und Frühchristentum², 2 vols. (Vienna; repr. Darmstadt, 1967).

Billault, A. (1991): 'Les formes romanesques de l'héroisation dans la *Vie d'Apollonios de Tyane*', *BAGB* 1991, 267–74.

—— (2000): *L'univers de Philostrate* (Bruxelles).

Billerbeck, M. and Zubler, C. (2000): *Das Lob der Fliege von Lukian bis L.B. Alberti* (Bern).

Bing, P. (2003): 'The Unruly Tongue: Philitas of Cos as Scholar and Poet', *CPh* 98, 330–48.

Blois, L. de (1986): 'The εἰς βασιλέα of Ps.-Aristides', *GRBS* 27, 279–88.

Bosworth, A.B. (1993): 'Arrian and Rome: The Minor Works', *ANRW* 2.34.1, 226–75.

Boulanger, A. (1923): *Aelius Aristide et la sophistique dans la province d'Asie au IIe siècle de notre ère* (Paris).

Bourdieu, P. (1977): *Outline of a Theory of Practice*, trans. R. Nice (Cambridge).

—— (1989): *Distinction: A Social Critique of the Judgement of Taste*, trans. R. Nice (London).

Bowersock, G.W. (1965): *Augustus and the Greek World* (Oxford).

—— (1969): *Greek Sophists in the Roman Empire* (Oxford).

—— ed. (1974): *Approaches to the Second Sophistic* (University Park, PA).

Bowie, E.L. and Harrison, S.J. (1993): 'The Romance of the Novel', *JRS* 83, 159–78.

Bowie, E.L. (1974): 'The Greeks and their Past in the Second Sophistic', in M.I. Finley ed., *Studies in Ancient Society* (London), 166–209 [revised from *P&P* 46 (1971), 3–41].

—— (1978): 'Apollonius of Tyana: Tradition and Reality', *ANRW* 2.16.2, 1652–99.

—— (1982): 'The Importance of Sophists', *YCS* 27, 29–59.

—— (1990): 'Greek Poetry in the Antonine Age', in D.A. Russell ed., *Antonine Literature* (Oxford), 53–90.

—— (1994): 'Philostratus: Writer of Fiction', in J. Morgan and R. Stoneman eds., *Greek Fiction: The Greek Novel in Context* (London), 181–99.

—— (2002a): 'Literary Activity in Achaea', in P.A. Stadter and L. van der Stockt eds., *Sage and Emperor: Plutarch, Greek Intellectuals, and Roman Power in the Time of Trajan* (Leuven), 41–56.

—— (2002b): 'The Chronology of the Earlier Greek Novels since B.E. Perry: Revisions and Precisions', *Ancient Narrative* 2, 47–63.

Bowman, A. and Woolf, G., eds. (1994): *Literacy and Power in the Ancient World* (Cambridge).

Branham, R.B. (1985): 'Introducing the Sophist: Lucian's Prologues', *TAPA* 115, 237–43.

—— (1989): *Unruly Eloquence: Lucian and the Comedy of Traditions* (Cambridge, MA).

Braund, D.C. and Wilkins, J.M., eds. (2000): *Athenaeus and his World: Reading Greek Culture in the Roman Empire* (Exeter).

Breitenbach, H.R. (1969): 'Der Alexanderexkurs bei Livius', *MH* 26, 146–57.

Bremen, R. van (1996): *The Limits of Participation: Women and Civic Life in the Greek East in the Hellenistic and Roman Periods* (Amsterdam).

Brown, P. (1978): *The Making of Late Antiquity* (Cambridge, MA).

—— (1989): *The Body and Society: Men, Women and Sexual Renunciation in Early Christianity* (London).

Brunt, P.A. (1994): 'The Bubble of the Second Sophistic', *BICS* 39, 25–52.

Cassin, B. (1986): 'Du faux ou du mensonge à la fiction', in B. Cassin ed., *Le plaisir du parler: études de sophistique comparée* (Paris), 3–29.

Clay, D. (1992): 'Four Philosophical Lives: (*Nigrinus, Demonax, Peregrinus, Alexander Pseudomantis*)', *ANRW* 2.36.5, 3406–50.

Cole, T. (1991): *The Origins of Rhetoric in Ancient Greece* (Baltimore).

Connolly, J. (2001): 'Reclaiming the Theatrical in the Second Sophistic', *Helios* 28, 75–96.

—— (2003): 'Like the Labours of Heracles: *andreia* and *paideia* in Greek Culture under Rome', in R.M. Rosen and I. Sluiter eds., *Andreia: Studies in Manliness and Courage in Classical Antiquity* (Leiden), 287–317.

Cooper, K. (1996): *The Virgin and the Bride: Idealized Womanhood in Late Antiquity* (Cambridge, MA).

Cox, P. (1983): *Biography in Late Antiquity: A Quest for the Holy Man* (Berkeley).

Cronje, J.V. (1993): 'The Principle of Concealment (ΤΟ ΛΑΘΕΙΝ) in Greek Literary Theory', *AClass* 36, 55–64.

Desideri P. (1978): *Dione di Prusa: un intelletuale greco nell' impero romano* (Messina).

Dodds, E.R. (1965): *Pagan and Christian in an Age of Anxiety* (Cambridge).

Dubel, S. (1994): 'Dialogue et autoportrait: les masques de Lucien', in A. Billault ed., *Lucien de Samosate* (Lyon), 19–26.

Duff, T.E. (1999): *Plutarch's Lives: Exploring Virtue and Vice* (Oxford).

Easterling, P. and Miles, R. (1999): 'Dramatic Identities: Tragedy in Late Antiquity', in R. Miles ed., *Constructing Identities in Late Antiquity* (London), 95–111.

Edwards, C. (1997): 'Self-scrutiny and Self-transformation in Seneca's *Letters*', *G&R* 44 (1997), 23–38.

Elsner, J. (1997): 'Hagiographic geography: Travel and Allegory in the *Life of Apollonius of Tyana*', *JHS* 117, 22–37.

Fears, J.R. (1974): 'The Stoic View of Alexander the Great', *Philologus* 118, 113–30.

Fein, S. (1994): *Die Beziehungen der Kaiser Trajan und Hadrian zu den Litterati* (Stuttgart).

Flinterman, J.-J. (1995): *Power, paideia & Pythagoreanism: Greek Identity, Conceptions of the Relationship between Philosophers and Monarchs and Political Ideas in Philostratus' Life of Apollonius* (Amsterdam).

Follet, S. (1991): 'Divers aspects de l'Hellénisme chez Philostrate', in S. Saïd ed., *ΕΛΛΗΝΙΣΜΟΣ: quelques jalons pour une histoire de l'identité grecque* (Leiden), 205–16.

Förster, R. (1893): *Scriptores physiognomonici graeci et latini*, 2 vols. (Leipzig).

Foucault, M. (1986): *The History of Sexuality. Vol. 3: The Care of the Self*, trans. R. Hurley (Harmondsworth).

Furley, W.D. and Bremer, J.M. (2001): *Greek Hymns: Selected Cult Songs from the Archaic to the Hellenistic Period*, 2 vols. (Tübingen).

Fusillo, M. (1988): 'Le miroir de la lune: l' "Histoire vraie" de Lucien, de la satire à l'utopie', *Poétique* 19/73, 109–35; translated as 'The Mirror of the Moon: Lucian's *A True Story*—from Satire to Utopia', in S. Swain ed., *Oxford Readings in the Greek Novel* (Oxford), 351–81.

Georgiadou, A. and Larmour, D.H.J. (1998): *Lucian's Science Fiction Novel True Histories: Interpretation and Commentary* (Leiden).

Gerth, K. (1956): 'Die zweite oder neue Sophistik', in *Paulys Real-Encyclopädie der classischen Altertumswissenschaft* supplementum VIII: 719–82.

Gleason, M.W. (1990): 'The Semiotics of Gender: Physiognomy and Self-fashioning in the Second Century C.E.', in D.M. Halperin, J.J. Winkler, and F.I. Zeitlin eds., *Before Sexuality: The Construction of Erotic Experience in the Ancient Greek World* (Princeton), 389–415.

—— (1995): *Making Men: Sophists and Self-presentation in Ancient Rome* (Princeton).

Goldhill, S.D. and Osborne, R., eds. (1999): *Performance Culture and Athenian Democracy* (Cambridge).

Goldhill, S.D. (1994): 'The Failure of Exemplarity', in I.F. de Jong and J.P. Sullivan eds., *Modern Critical Theory and Classical Literature* (Leiden), 51–73.

—— (1995): *Foucault's Virginity: Ancient Erotic Fiction and the History of Sexuality* (Cambridge).

—— ed. (2001): *Being Greek under Rome: The Second Sophistic, Cultural Conflict and the Development of the Roman Empire* (Cambridge).

—— (2002a): *The Invention of Prose, G&R* New Surveys in the Classics (Oxford).

—— (2002b): *Who Needs Greek? Contests in the Cultural History of Hellenism* (Cambridge).

Gruen, E. (1984): *The Hellenistic World and the Coming of Rome*, 2 vols. (Berkeley).

Gunderson, E. (2000): *Staging Masculinity: The Rhetoric of Performance in the Roman World* (Ann Arbor).

Guthrie, W.K.C. (1971): *The Sophists* (Cambridge).

Habicht, C. (1969): *Die Inschriften des Asklepieions: Altertümer von Pergamon* 8.3 (Berlin).

Hadas-Lebel, M. (1993): 'Le double récit autobiographique chez Flavius Josèphe', in M.-F. Baslez, P. Hoffmann, and L. Pernot eds., *L'invention de l'autobiographie d'Hésiode à Saint Angustine: actes du deuxième colloque de l'Équipe de recherche sur l'hellénisme post-classique* (Paris), 125–32.

Hadjú, K. (1998): *Ps.-Herodian, De figuris: Überlieferungsgeschichte und kritische Ausgabe* (Berlin).

Halfmann, H. (1979): *Die Senatoren aus dem östlichen Teil des Imperium romanum bis zum Ende des 2 Jh. n. Chr.* (Göttingen).

Hallett, J. (1993): 'Feminist Theory, Historical Periods, Literary Canons, and the Study of Greco-Roman Antiquity', in N. Rabinowitz and A. Richlin eds., *Feminist Theory and the Classics* (London), 44–72.

Hamilton, J.R. (1969): *Plutarch's Alexander: A Commentary* (Oxford).

Hansen, D.U. (1998): *Die attizistische Lexicon des Moeris: Quellenkritische Untersuchung und Edition* (Berlin).

Harris, W.V. (1989): *Ancient Literacy* (Cambridge, MA).

Harrison, S.J. (2000): *Apuleius: A Latin Sophist* (Oxford).

Hartog, F. (1991): 'Rome et la Grèce: les choix de Denys d'Halicarnasse', in S. Saïd ed., *EΛΛΗΝΙΣΜΟΣ: quelques jalons pour une histoire de l'identité grecque* (Leiden), 149–67.

Heath, M. (2004): *Menander: A Rhetor in Context* (Oxford).

Hesk, J. (2000): *Deception and Democracy in Classical Athens* (Cambridge).

Hidber, T. (1996): *Das klassizistische Manifest des Dionys von Halikarnass: die Praefatio zu "De oratoribus veteribus": Einleitung, Übersetzung, und Kommentar* (Stuttgart).

Higgins, M.J. (1945): 'The Renaissance of the First Century and the Origin of Standard Late Greek', *Traditio* 3, 47–100.

Hinck, H. (1873): *Polemonis declamationes quae exstant duae* (Leipzig).

Höistad, R. (1948): *Cynic Hero and Cynic King: Studies in the Cynic Conception of Man* (Uppsala).

Holford-Strevens, L. (1997): 'Favorinus: The Man of Paradoxes', in J. Barnes and M. Griffin eds., *Philosophia togata II: Plato and Aristotle at Rome* (Oxford), 188–217.

—— (2003): *Aulus Gellius: An Antonine Scholar and his Achievement*[2] (Oxford).

Hopkins, K. (1965): 'Elite Mobility in the Roman Empire', *P&P* 32 (1965), 12–26; repr. in M.I. Finley ed., *Studies in Ancient Society* (London, 1974), 103–20.

Horrocks, G. (1997): *Greek: A History of the Language and its Speakers* (London).

Humbert, S. (1991): 'Plutarque, Alexandre et l'hellénisme', in S. Saïd ed., *ΕΛΛΗΝΙΣΜΟΣ: quelques jalons pour une histoire de l'identité grecque* (Leiden), 169–82.

Hunter, R.L. (1983): *A Study of* Daphnis and Chloe (Cambridge).

Jeanneret, M. (1991): *A Feast of Words: Banquets and Table-talk in the Renaissance*, trans. J. Whiteley and E. Hughes (Cambridge).

Jenkyns, R. (1980): *The Victorians and Ancient Greece* (Oxford).

Jones, C.P. (1971): *Plutarch and Rome* (Oxford).

—— (1972): 'Aelius Aristides, εἰς βασιλέα', *JRS* 62, 134–52.

—— (1974): 'The Reliability of Philostratus', in G.W. Bowersock ed., *Approaches to the Second Sophistic* (University Park, PA), 11–16.

—— (1978): *The Roman World of Dio Chrysostom* (Cambridge, MA).

—— (1981): 'The εἰς βασιλέα Again', *CQ* 31, 224–5.

—— (1986): *Culture and Society in Lucian* (Cambridge, MA).

—— (1991): 'Dinner Theatre', in W.J. Slater ed., *Dining in a Classical Context* (Ann Arbor), 185–98.

—— (2002): 'Philostratus and the Gordiani', *Mediterraneo Antico* 5, 759–67.

Jouan, F. (2002): 'Mensonges d'Ulysse, mensonges d'Homère', *REG* 115, 409–16.

Kayser, C.L. (1871): *Flavii Philostrati Opera*, vol. II (Leipzig).

Keil, J. (1953): 'Vertreter der zweiten Sophistik in Ephesos', *JÖAI* 40, 5–26.

Kennedy, G.A. (1974): 'The sophists as declaimers', in G.W. Bowersock ed., *Approaches to the Second Sophistic* (University Park, PA), 17–22.

—— (1994): *A New History of Classical Rhetoric* (Princeton).

Kennell, N.M. (1988): 'ΝΕΡΩΝ ΠΕΡΙΟΔΟΝΙΚΗΣ', *AJP* 109, 239–51.

—— (1997): 'Herodes Atticus and the Rhetoric of Tyranny', *CPh* 92, 346–62.

Kerferd, G.B. (1981): *The Sophistic Movement* (Cambridge).

Kiehr, F. (1906): *Lesbonactis sophistae quae supersunt* (Strasburg).

Kindstrand, J.F. (1973): *Homer in der zweiten Sophistik* (Uppsala).

Kohl, R. (1915): *De scholasticarum declamationum argumentis ex historia petitis* (Diss. Paderborn).

König, J.P. (2001): 'Favorinus' *Corinthian Oration* in its Corinthian Context', *PCPS* 47, 141–71.

—— (forthcoming): *Athletics and Literature in the Roman Empire* (Cambridge).

Konstan, D. and Saïd, S., eds. (forthcoming): *Greeks on Greekness: The Construction and Uses of the Greek Past among Greeks under the Roman Empire*, *PCPS* Supplementary Vol. (Cambridge).

Konstan, D. (1994): *Sexual Symmetry: Love in the Ancient Novel and Related Genres* (Princeton).

Korenjak, M. (2000): *Publikum und Redner: ihre Interaktion in der sophistischen Rhetorik der Kaiserzeit* (Munich).

—— (2003): 'Homer und die sophistische Rhetorik der Kaiserzeit', *MH* 60, 129–45.

Körner, C.A. (2002): 'Die Rede *Eis basilea* des Pseudo-Aelius Aristides', *MH* 59, 211–28.

Koskenniemi, E. (1991): *Der philostrateische Apollonios* (Helsinki).

Lane Fox, R. (1986): *Pagans and Christians* (London).

Lannoy, L. de (1997): 'Le problème des Philostrate (état de la question)', *ANRW* 2.34.3, 2362–449.

Lewis, N. (1981): 'Literati in the Service of Roman Emperors: Politics before Culture', in L. Casson and M. Price eds., *Coins, Culture and History in the Ancient World: Numismatic and Other Studies in Honor of Bluma L. Trell* (Detroit), 149–66; repr. in N. Lewis, *On Government and Law in Roman Egypt* (Atlanta, 1995), 257–74.

Librale, D. (1994): 'L' εἰς βασιλέα dello pseudo-Aristide e l'ideologia traianea', *ANRW* 2.34.2, 1271–313.

Lightfoot, J.L. (2003): *Lucian, On the Syrian Goddess: Edited with Introduction, Translation, and Commentary* (Oxford).

Long, A.A. (2002): *Epictetus: A Stoic and Socratic Guide to Life* (Oxford).

Macdowell, D.M. (1982): *Gorgias, Encomium of Helen* (Bristol).

Marrou, H. (1956): *A History of Education in Antiquity*, trans. G. Lamb (London).

Martindale, C. (1993): *Redeeming the Text: Latin Poetry and the Hermeneutics of Reception* (Cambridge).

Mason, H. (1974): *Greek Terms for Roman Institutions* (Toronto).

McArthur, T. (1986): *Worlds of Reference: Lexicography, Learning and Language from the Clay Tablet to the Computer* (Cambridge).

Millar, F. (1977): *The Emperor in the Roman World 31 BC–AD 337* (London).

Misch, G. (1950): *A History of Autobiography in Antiquity*, 2 vols. (London).

Mitchell, S. (1990): 'Festivals, Games and Civic Life In Roman Asia Minor', *JRS* 80, 183–93.

Moles J.L. (1978): 'The Career and Conversion of Dio Chrysostom', *JHS* 98, 79–100.

—— (1990): 'The *Kingship Orations* of Dio Chrysostom', *Papers of the Leeds Latin Seminar* 6, 297–375.

—— (forthcoming): 'The 13th *Oration* of Dio Chrysostom: Complexity and Simplicity', *JHS*.

Möllendorff, P. von (2000): *Auf der Suche nach der verlogenen Wahrheit: Lukians Wahre Geschichten* (Tübingen).

Momigliano, A. (1993): *The Development of Greek Biography*, expanded edition (Cambridge, MA).

Morgan, T. (1998): *Literate Education in the Hellenistic and Roman Worlds* (Cambridge).

—— (1999): 'Literate Education in Classical Athens', *CQ* 49, 46–61.

Nesselrath, H.-G. (1990): 'Lucian's Introductions', in D.A. Russell ed., *Antonine Literature* (Oxford), 111–40.

—— (1998): Review of Schmitz (1997): *BMCR* 1998/98.6.18 (archived at ⟨http://ccat.sas.upenn.edu/bmcr/1998/98.6.18.html⟩).

Nietzsche, F. (1993): *The Birth of Tragedy out of the Spirit of Music*, trans. S. Whiteside (London).

Nijf, O. van (1999): 'Athletics, Festivals and Greek Identity in the Roman East', *PCPS* 45, 175–200.

—— (2001): 'Local Heroes: Athletics, Festivals and Elite Self-fashioning in the Roman East', in S.D. Goldhill ed., *Being Greek under Rome: Cultural Identity, the Second Sophistic and the Development of Empire* (Cambridge), 306–34.

—— (2003): 'Athletics, *andreia* and the *askēsis* Culture in the Roman East', in R.M. Rosen and I. Sluiter eds., *Andreia: Studies in Manliness and Courage in Classical Antiquity* (Leiden), 263–86.

Norden, E. (1898): *Die antike Kunstprosa vom VI. Jahrhundert v. Chr. bis in die Zeit der Renaissance*, 2 vols. (Leipzig; repr. Stuttgart, 1971).

Nutton, V. (1970): 'Herodes and Gordian', *Latomus* 29, 719–28.

Oliver, J.H. (1968): *The Civilizing Power: A Study of the* Panathenaic Discourse *of Aelius Aristides against the Background of Literature and Cultural Conflict, with Text, Translation, and Commentary* (Philadelphia).

Osborne, R. (1985): 'Law and Action in Classical Athens', *JHS* 105, 40–58.

Papalas, A.J. (1978): 'Lucius Verus and the Hospitality of Herodes Atticus', *Athenaeum* 56, 182–5.

Pearcy, L.T. (1988): 'Theme, Dream and Narrative: Reading the *Sacred Tales* of Aelius Aristides', *TAPA* 118, 377–91.

—— (1993): 'Medicine and Rhetoric in the Period of the Second Sophistic', *ANRW* 2.37.1, 445–56.

Pelling, C.B.R. (1995): 'The Moralism of Plutarch's *Lives*', in D. Innes, H. Hine, and C.B.R. Pelling eds., *Ethics and Rhetoric: Classical Essays for Donald Russell on his Seventy-fifth Birthday* (Oxford), 205–20; reprinted at Pelling (2002), 237–51.

—— (2002): *Plutarch and History: Eighteen Studies* (Swansea).

Perkins, J. (1995): *The Suffering Self: Pain and Narrative Representation in the Early Christian Era* (London).

Pernot, L. (1993): *La rhétorique de l'éloge dans le monde gréco-romain*, 2 vols. (Paris).

Price, S.R.F. (1984): *Rituals and Power: The Roman Imperial Cult in Asia Minor* (Cambridge).

Puech, B. (2002): *Orateurs et sophistes grecs dans les inscriptions d'époque impériale* (Paris).

Quet, M.H. (1993): 'Parler de soi pour louer son dieu: le cas d'Aelius Aristide (du journal intime de ses nuits aux *Discours sacrés* en l'honneur du dieu Asklepios)', in M.-F. Baslez, P. Hoffmann, and L. Pernot eds., *L'Invention de l'autobiographie d'Hésiode à Saint Augustine: actes du deuxiéme colloque de l'Équipe de recherche sur l'hellénisme post-classique* (Paris), 211–51.

Reader, W.W. (1996): *The Severed Hand and the Upright Corpse: The Declamations of Marcus Antonius Polemo* (Atlanta).

Reardon, B.P. (1971): *Courants littéraires grecs des IIe et IIIe siècles après J.-C.* (Paris).

—— (1974): 'The Second Sophistic and the Novel', in G.W. Bowersock ed., *Approaches to the Second Sophistic* (University Park, PA), 23–9.

Rohde, E. (1886): 'Die asianische Rhetorik und die zweite Sophistik', *RhM* 41, 170–90; repr. in *Kleine Schriften* 2 (Tübingen, 1901), 75–97.

—— (1914): *Der griechische Roman und seine Vorläufer*[3], rev. W. Schmid (Leipzig; repr. Hildesheim, 1960).

Rothe, S. (1989): *Kommentar zu ausgewählten Sophistenvitae des Philostratos: die Lehrstuhlinhaber in Athen und Rom* (Heidelberg).

Russell, D.A. and Wilson, N.G. (1981): *Menander Rhetor: Edited with Translation and Commentary* (Oxford).

Russell, D.A. (1972): *Plutarch* (London).

—— (1981): *Criticism in Antiquity* (London).

—— (1983): *Greek Declamation* (Cambridge).

Rutherford, I. (1995): 'The Poetics of the *paraphthegma*: Aelius Aristides and the *decorum* of Self-praise', in D.C. Innes, H.M. Hine, and C.B.R. Pelling eds., *Ethics and Rhetoric: Classical Essays for Donald Russell on his Seventy-fifth Birthday* (Oxford), 193–204.

—— (1998): *Canons of Style in the Antonine Age: Idea-theory in its Literary Context* (Oxford).

Rutherford, J., ed. (1990): *Identity* (London).

Rütten, U. (1997): *Phantasie und Lachkultur: Lukians* Wahre Geschichten (Tübingen).

Saïd, S. (1993): 'Le "je" de Lucien', in M.-F. Baslez, P. Hoffmann, and L. Pernot eds., *L'Invention de l'autobiographie d'Hésiode à Saint Augustine: actes du deuxiéme colloque de l'Équipe de recherche sur l'hellénisme post-classique* (Paris), 211–51.

—— (2000): 'Dio's Use of Mythology', in S. Swain ed., *Dio Chrysostom: Politics, Letters, and Philosophy* (Oxford), 161–86.

Sandbach, F.H. (1936): 'Atticism and the Second Sophistic Movement', in *The Cambridge Ancient History*[1], 11, 678–90.

Scardigli, B., ed. (1995): *Essays in Plutarch's* Lives (Oxford).

Schmeling, G., ed. (2003): *The Novel in the Ancient World*[2] (Leiden).

Schmid, W. (1887–96): *Der Atticismus in seinen Hauptvertretern von Dionysius von Halikarnass bis auf den zweiten Philostratus*, 4 vols., (Stuttgart).

Schmitz, T. (1997): *Bildung und Macht: zur sozialen unde politischen Funktion der zweiten Sophistik in der griechischen Welt der Kaiserzeit* (Munich).

—— (forthcoming): 'Narrator and Audience in Philostratus' *Lives of the Sophists*', in E.L. Bowie and J. Elsner eds., *Philostratus* (Cambridge).

Schröder, S. (1991): 'Zu Plutarchs Alexanderreden', *MH* 48 (1991), 151–7.

Schwartz, J. (1965): *Biographie de Lucien de Samosate* (Brussels).

Solin, H. (2001): 'Latin cognomina in the Greek East', in O. Salomies ed., *The Greek East in the Roman Context: Proceedings of a Colloquium Organised by the Finnish Institute at Athens, May 21 and 22 1999* (Helsinki), 189–202.

Sordi, M. (1982): 'Timagene: uno storico ellenocentrico e filobarbaro', *ANRW* 2.30.1, 775–97.

Spawforth, A.J. (1980): 'Sparta and the Family of Herodes Atticus: A Reconstruction of the Evidence', *BSA* 75, 203–20.

Staden, H. von (1997): 'Galen and the "Second Sophistic" ', in R. Sorabji ed., *Aristotle and After* (London), 33–54.

Stadter, P.A. (1980): *Arrian of Nicomedia* (Chapel Hill).

Stanton, G.R. (1973): 'Sophists and Philosophers: Problems of Classification', *AJP* 94, 350–64.

Stephens, S.A. and Winkler, J.J. (1995): *Ancient Greek Novels, the Fragments: Introduction, Text, Translation, and Commentary* (Princeton).

Stertz, S.A. (1979): 'Pseudo-Aristides, εἰς βασιλέα', *CQ* 29, 172–97.

Stray, C. (1998): *Classics Transformed: Schools, Universities and Society in England, 1830–1960* (Oxford).

Sturrock, J. (1993): *The Language of Autobiography: Studies in the First Person Singular* (Cambridge).

Swain, S.C.R. and Edwards, M.J., eds. (1997): *Portraits: Biographical Representation in the Greek and Latin Literature of the Roman Empire* (Oxford).

Swain, S.C.R. (1989): 'Plutarch's *De fortuna Romanorum*', *CQ* 39, 504–16.

—— (1991): 'The Reliability of Philostratus' *Lives of the Sophists*', *ClAnt* 10, 148–63.

—— (1996): *Hellenism and Empire: Language, Classicism, and Power in the Greek World, AD 50–250* (Oxford).

—— (1997): 'Biography and Biographic in the Literature of the Roman Empire', in Swain and Edwards, eds. (1997), 1–37.

—— (1999): 'Defending Hellenism: Philostratus, *In Honour of Apollonius*', in M. Edwards, M. Goodman, and S. Price eds., *Apologetics in the Roman Empire: Pagans, Jews and Christians* (Oxford), 157–96.

—— ed. (1999): *Oxford Readings in the Greek Novel* (Oxford).

Syme, R. (1982): *Greeks Invading the Roman Government* (Brookline); repr. in A. Birley ed., *Roman papers* IV (Oxford, 1988), 1–20.

Tirelli, A. (1995): 'L'intelletuale e il potere: pedagogia e politica in Plutarco', in I. Gallo and B. Scardigli eds., *Teoria e prassi politica nelle opere di Plutarco. Atti del V convegno plutarcheo (Certosa di Pontignano 7–9 giugno 1993)* (Naples), 439–55.

Tobin, J. (1997): *Herodes Attikos and the City of Athens: Patronage and Conflict under the Antonines* (Amsterdam).

Tonnet, H. (1988): *Recherches sur Arrien: sa personnalité et ses écrits atticistes*, 2 vols. (Amsterdam).

Too, Y.L., ed. (2001): *Education in Greek and Roman Antiquity* (Leiden).

Toohey, P. (2004): *Melancholy, Love, and Time: Boundaries of the Self in Ancient Literature* (Michigan).

Tordesillas A. (1986): 'L'instance temporelle dans l'argumentation de la première et de la seconde sophistique: la notion de *kairos*', in B. Cassin ed., *Le plaisir de parler: études de sophistique comparée* (Paris), 31–61.

Turner, F.M. (1981): *The Greek Heritage in Victorian Britain* (New Haven).

Usher, S. (1993): 'Isocrates: *paideia*, Kingship and the Barbarians', in H.A. Khan ed., *The Birth of the European Identity: The Europe–Asia Contrast in Greek Thought* (Nottingham), 131–45.

Veyne, P. (1978): 'La famille et l'amour sous le Haut-Empire romain', *Annales E.S.C.* 33, 35–63; repr. as *La société romaine* (Paris, 1991), 88–130.

Victor, U. (1997): *Lukian, Alexandros oder Der Lügenprophet* (Leiden).

Vidal-Naquet, P. (1984): 'Flavius Arrien entre deux mondes', in P. Savinel trans., *Arrien, Histoire d'Alexandre* (Paris), 311–94.

Volkmann, R. (1885): *Die Rhetorik der Griechen und Römer in systematischer Übersicht*[2] (Leipzig; repr. Hildesheim, 1963).

Walker, S. and Cameron, A., eds. (1989): *The Greek Renaissance in the Roman Empire: Papers from the Tenth British Museum Colloquium* (London).

Wardy, R.B. (1996): *The Birth of Rhetoric: Gorgias, Plato, and their Successors* (London).

Weissenberger, M. (1996): *Literaturtheorie bei Lukian: Untersuchung zum Dialog 'Lexiphanes'* (Stuttgart).

Whitmarsh, T. (1998): 'Reading Power in Roman Greece: The *paideia* of Dio Chrysostom', in Y.L. Too and N. Livingstone eds., *Pedagogy and Power: Rhetorics of Classical Learning* (Cambridge), 192–213.

—— (2001): *Greek Literature and the Roman Empire: The Politics of Imitation* (Oxford).

—— (2002): 'Alexander's Hellenism and Plutarch's Textualism', *CQ* 52, 174–92.

—— (2004a): *Ancient Greek Literature* (Cambridge).

—— (2004b): 'The Cretan Lyre Paradox: Mesomedes, Hadrian and the Poetics of Patronage', in B. Borg ed., *Paideia: The World of the Second Sophistic* (Berlin), 359–76.

—— (2004c): 'Philostratus', in I.J.F. de Jong, R. Nünlist, and A. Bowie eds., *Narrators, Narratees, and Narratives in Ancient Greek Literature* (Leiden), 423–39.

—— (2004d): 'Dio Chrysostom', in I.J.F. de Jong, R. Nünlist, and A. Bowie eds., *Narrators, Narratees, and Narratives in Ancient Greek Literature* (Leiden), 451–64.

—— (2004e): 'Lucian', in I.J.F. de Jong, R. Nünlist, and A. Bowie eds., *Narrators, Narratees, and Narratives in Ancient Greek Literature* (Leiden), 465–76.

—— (2004f): 'Aristides', in I.J.F. de Jong, R. Nünlist, and A. Bowie eds., *Narrators, Narratees, and Narratives in Ancient Greek Literature* (Leiden), 441–7.

Wilamowitz (1900): = Wilamowitz-Möllendorff, U. von: 'Asianismus und Atticismus', *Hermes* 35, 1–52; repr. in *Kleine Schriften* 3 (Berlin, 1969), 223–73.

Winkler, J.J. (1980): 'Lollianos and the Desperadoes', *JHS* 100, 155–81.

—— (1990): *The Constraints of Desire: The Anthropology of Sex and Gender in the Ancient World* (New York).

Woolf, G. (1994): 'Becoming Roman, Staying Greek: Culture, Identity and the Civilizing Process in the Roman East', *PCPS* 40, 116–43.

Wright, W.C. (1921): *Philostratus and Eunapius, Lives of the Sophists* (Cambridge, MA).

ABOUT THE AUTHOR

Tim Whitmarsh is Reader in Greek at the University of Exeter. A specialist in the Greek literature of the Roman Empire, he has published widely, including: Greek Literature and the Roman Empire: the Politics of Imitation (Oxford, 2001), Achilles Tatius: Leucippe and Clitophon, Translated with Notes (Oxford, 2001), and Ancient Greek Literature (Cambridge, 2004).

INDEX

Names are given in their simplest and most conventional form. Fuller forms (ethnonyms, *praenomina*, descriptions etc.) are only given in cases of potential ambiguity.